WRITERS REPUBLIC

Your Cuppa Tea

LINDSAY MAXWELL

WRITERS REPUBLIC L.L.C.
515 Summit Ave. Unit R1
Union City, NJ 07087, USA

Website: *www.writersrepublic.com*
Hotline: *1-877-656-6838*
Email: *info@writersrepublic.com*

Ordering Information:
Quantity sales. Special discounts are available on quantity purchases by corporations, associations, and others. For details, contact the publisher at the address above.

Library of Congress Control Number: 2022950311
ISBN-13:   979-8-88536-113-2   [Paperback Edition]
                  979-8-88536-114-9   [Digital Edition]

Rev. date: 11/22/2022

For my sister, Suzanne...
Whom I always enjoy "tea tea" time with.

I am free.

I awoke from a dream last night. If you've been following my writing for a number of years now, you'll note that I often have prophetic and/or impactful dreams that have messages. It's something I never delved into too deeply, but it intrigues me just the same.

My dream whispered to me last night that there is freedom in forgiveness.

I cannot stress enough how very true that is.

Forgiving someone or something can be very difficult, indeed, especially when you feel that you were the one who was slighted or on the receiving end of their negative emotions and reactions.

However, no matter how deep the sadness dwells, you will not be free of them until there is forgiveness in your heart.

It does not mean that what they did makes it okay. It does not mean that you have to be besties with them. And—this is the hard one—you may have moments of forgiveness and then loathe them afterward down the road and have to start all over with your cycle of forgiving.

I learned this lesson swiftly years ago that the only way to move forward from events and people who have hurt you is to forgive. It may take longer than you want sometimes. But it's a way through.

My encouragement for you (because we all have people in our lives that we could be thinking about right now as I write these words) is to write a little letter that you need not send to a person, whether still living or not, who has hurt you. You may write the words "I forgive you" just to see how that feels. Note your feelings upon writing it.

For all my '80s movie lovers out there who remember the scene from *Labyrinth* where Sarah told the Goblin King, "You have no power over me," this one is for you.

Freedom.

Love,

Lindsay Maxwell

I had a strange moment happen not too long ago.

A minor upset happened, and I was feeling the aftermath of it. I went for a walk in my neighborhood as it was a beauty of a day. I was totally in my head stewing, and a man crossed my path, and with a warm and genuine smile he said, "I really hope you a spectacular day. I truly do."

And then he went about his way.

This man was a complete stranger, and the energy he emitted was radiant and lovely.

Well, that snapped me out of my funk immediately. After that quick encounter, I started to look around me—the leaves starting to fall, the brightness of the sunshine, and the contrasts of light.

I then thought to myself that that man came right at the perfect moment. It's almost like the Man Upstairs knew I needed a wee pick-me-up and sent an Earth angel to come just at the right time.

Even though it was something minor, I took it as something profound. We are provided for. We are taken care of.

We just need to pay attention.

It's all in the details.

I'm very thankful for the little moments and the big moments. That is what life is composed of.

Enjoy your moments, loved ones.

With extra gravy,

Lindsay Maxwell

It's okay to not be okay.

As humans, we strive to feel okay. We eat healthy and exercise to feel okay. We have careers to earn an income so that we feel okay. We meet up with friends and family and tell jokes and stories so that we feel okay. We take to finding a romantic partner so that we can feel okay. We pray, meditate, and ground ourselves so that we can feel okay.

But sometimes we just don't feel okay. And . . . that's okay.

We are setting ourselves up for immeasurable disappointment if we are always chasing a feeling of being okay.

Sometimes, for no reason at all, we are full of exuberance. And sometimes when the world is at our fingertips and everything is going seemingly right, we feel a sadness dwelling within us.

I know we want to feel good. That is the ideal. And yes, striving to feel well in areas of your life is great and a good goal to have.

But . . . we have that thing in common with each other. We are humans. And humans have these things called emotions. And sometimes emotions don't always line up with how we think we *should* be feeling.

And sometimes things are just not okay. Not at all. And it's soul crushing. It can hurt terribly and spark something within us we did not even know we possessed.

Hence, we are able to feel everything from rage, peace, depression, and utter joy to the whole git and gamble. We are all from different environments, families, experiences, thought processes, hormone levels, temperaments, etc.

Cut yourself some slack. If you're not feeling okay . . . that's okay, because, dear reader, one day you will again.

The sun will rise, and the sun will set. And within your day and within your life you will have many moments; and you will surpass, surplus, and maybe even surf.

My encouragement for you is to breathe in and out. That's it. Deep breaths. There you go. I feel you. I see you.

Sending love to that heart of yours,

Lindsay Maxwell

Your soul knows.

If your intuition has been questioning things and something just feels off about a person or situation or topic, it is good to delve deeper into that.

You see, you and I are made from love.

We have virtue, truth, harmony, goodness, strength, hope, and forgiveness woven all within us.

But as humans in this all too topsy-turvy of a world, we can tend to lose sight of what we innately are and what we intrinsically know.

Remember, my dear reader, if it doesn't bear good fruit, is the foundation and soil good?

My gentle encouragement for you is to take a hard look and question your own perspective. I actually actively do this often to make sure that I'm not too rigid in always believing my own narrative. Just because you believed something so strongly before, don't feel as though you can't grow out of it and shed some of those beliefs now. There is no shame in growth and change, especially as it brings you closer to love and truth.

Your soul knows. Listen and honor it.

With great love,

Lindsay Maxwell

You do you.

I'll do me.

I am certainly not blind to seeing the consistent tug-of-war as of late on our media.

Something popped into my head last night. No matter the fighting, division, name-calling, bantering, finger-pointing, shaming, etc., one does, you're probably not going to change another person's views or innate nature.

That stuff takes a desire from said person to change. And a knowledge that one is in need of change. And that, my friends, can take years of discipline and self-awareness. Or not.

Now, I am pro educating, guiding, gentle nudging, setting a good example, listening, storytelling, sharing, compassion, and just plumb empathy.

I am very in tune with all sorts of feelings; it derives from being an actress, writer, and hairstylist. There is *nothing* I haven't heard, examined, studied (character study), or really felt myself.

What I am observing are a lot of people's surface "go-to's." If you have anger/fear/resentment on the tip of your heart, you're going to be more readily available to act out from that.

Those are all human emotions, yes, but they're rather unpleasant to dwell in. I know we are being tested beyond our comprehension, so it's no wonder the world feels more topsy-turvy as of late.

My gentle encouragement for you is to do a wee bit of digging into your psyche. If you find yourself ready to fight and judge and shame, ask yourself why. If you're feeling anxious and nervous, get to the root of it and perhaps call someone to talk.

And if you're happy and you know it, clap your hands.

Applauding to your growth and your desire to reflect. You're doing well, kiddo.

Love,

Lindsay Maxwell

Build a life that you don't need a vacation from.

I often write about our "grand mural" of life. You are a beautiful masterpiece. You have all the colors. Even the ones you like the least. But you need all the colors to contrast the light and fill in with shading.

Stepping back, you'll see your mural is beautiful and profound. Yet if you look at it up close, you may find an area where there is a lot of darkness. Close by though, dear reader, is a glimmer of light. This I promise you.

Vacationing and traveling are wonderful things. They provide a change of scenery and add a richness and awareness to your life. It offers different customs, languages, culinary delights, and a myriad of other little goodies. Upon returning home, you've changed yet are still the same. Things look . . . different.

But home is where the heart is. And that is where we are grounded.

My challenge and encouragement for you today is to reflect on where you are at in your home life. Are you nurturing your loved ones? Are you taking enough quality time for yourself? Are you doing nice things as a family? Are you unplugging and having a games night? Even if you're single, do you make time to see friends? Volunteer?

Build a life that you don't need to feel you need to escape from.

As Ms. Dorothy Gale once said, "If I ever go looking for my heart's desire again, I won't look any further than my own backyard. Because if it isn't there, I never really lost it to begin with. There's no place like home."

Clicking my heels,

Lindsay Maxwell

Your lack of forgiveness is going to hurt.

Oh, we have all had terrible and inexplicable events and trauma that have happened. We have things that have occurred in our lives that make our core shudder and leave us with deep scars.

I do not pretend to know the aches and pains of your journey. But I know in this life, unjust situations can and will happen.

To have this experience on Earth is to go through beauty, sadness, pain, redemption, loss, betrayal, gratitude, lessons, and every other descriptive word you could insert here.

We all know that quote, "Holding on to anger is like drinking poison expecting the other person to die."

It's true.

Dear reader, I know it gets hard. I know you were wronged. Maybe you couldn't fight back. Maybe you didn't have a voice. Maybe there are just some things that are unforgivable.

I recently reread one of my favorite books called *The Shack*.

There is a lot of reference to a journey of forgiveness.

Forgiving doesn't mean forgetting. Forgiving doesn't mean that you need a relationship or friendship with your perpetrator.

I will share some insight on how I try to work through some things myself.

First, I pray. I ask for the heart behind forgiving.

Second, I am an artist and an empath. I try to look at the big picture. Does this person come from a broken childhood? Is this person struggling with their own demons?

You see, hurt people *hurt* people.

My gentle encouragement for you today (respectively, wherever you are at on your journey) is for you to find a quiet place in your heart to forgive a wrongdoing, big or small. It may be a one-time thing. Or it may take you to a place where you have to remind yourself to forgive every day.

It will help with your freedom.

With a loving hug as I know it was a heavy one today,

Lindsay Maxwell

What is love?

Is it sacrifice? Is it a feeling? Is it choosing to commit when all seems lost? Is it putting someone before yourself? Is it madness? Is it sacred? Is it intangible? Is it pure? Is it life giving? Is it unexplainable at times? Is it even necessary?

Oh, my dear readers, it is all of the above, and then throw in 1 Corinthians to boot, and you have yourself a big love fest.

Love is in every corner of life. It is within each person I have crossed. It is shown by strangers, family, and friends who are like family. Love is in the sight of a cherry blossom tree. It is woven within a conversation between old friends. It is tangled up with you on Sunday morning. It is French toast with coffee and your lover. It is family outings. It is sitting by her hospital bed and holding her hand. It is supporting him emotionally when he feels all is lost. It is taking your ailing parent on a drive to see the neighborhood they grew up in . . .

Love is a verb. It's an act of devotion even when we do not feel as though we have it in us to give.

It is the most talked about subject on this planet. It creates the greatest highs, and the loss of a loved one can deliver some of the deepest sorrows.

But, my dear ones, we are equipped with a resilient heart. We come from love, and that is what we innately are intended to do: love.

My challenge for you is to act out of love in each corner of your life. Go the extra mile with someone who needs help. Call up your friend and go for a walk. Kiss your spouse mid-argument and have a wee laugh at the absurdity of it all. Pay attention to the details.

Love is something if you give it away.

Eat your heart out and fill 'er up,

We all have a story within that we don't share.

Are we fearful to let others in? If so, why?

Is it because we feel vulnerable to the way they could potentially make us feel? Are we scared of feeling judged? Is there a certain responsibility and accountability once you cross a threshold of drawing close to another?

What I know from deep within is that I am so grateful to have developed strong, deep, and loyal friendships and relationships with others that have stood the test of time.

We are built and wired to not go at this life alone.

I was chatting with someone yesterday about life. I was sharing with them some personal experiences I have had in the past year. They were loving and empathetic and commenting on my strength and ability to handle myself in a manner which they stated that they didn't think they would have the capacity to if they found themselves to be faced in my position.

I responded with this:

"God knew what I was going to go through, and he made sure that I would be surrounded by Earth angels and people to lift me up every step of the way. And though I rely on God's strength, I feel eternally fortunate the relationships that I have forged with others were there to guide me through some of my darkest hours."

We all have different chapters and stories and plot twists woven into our lives. Some are too strong of a burden to carry alone.

My challenge and encouragement for you is to reflect on nurturing your relationships, friendships, and family. Build a solid and strong foundation with them. We are here to get close, lean on, and support one another during our trials and tribulations. It's okay to need help. It's okay to ask. And you can be their help as well.

Tell your story. You never know who can relate and whom you can assist with on their journey.

With love,

Lindsay Maxwell

Know your roots.

I have often touted that at any moment we can change, we are not defined by our past, and we are meant to live in the moment.

While all of this is true, there is still something vital and poignant about knowing where we have come from and how we carry that throughout our lives.

Most of us have had a certain type of structure in how we got to this exact second today. You had early education, played with toys, got bullied, learned mathematics, and had an upbringing. All of this shaped and formed you during your beginning years.

You grew from that. You branched out. You leaved.

And here you are. Blooming away.

I know, dear reader, that not all of you had a happy and carefree childhood. I know that some of you wish you could go back and change something from your past or upbringing.

But . . . your foundation and formation has led you here and now today. You are a product of where you came from and now are on a "choose your own adventure" quest.

However, the nostalgia that you may feel from days of yore is there to remind you of that child who still dwells within. The child who seeks adventure, innocence, growth, and lessons.

Yes, even if you are ninety-three and reading this, there is that child (your root) who is still just as vibrant and pulsating as ever and wanting to create something big or small.

You came from innate love and are here to love. Nothing more. Nothing less. Just a little bit ride or die in between.

My challenge and encouragement for you today is to take a moment and reminisce of what that root of you wants and desires. Are you operating from there? Are you feeling connected? Do you remember where you came from?

With rootin' tootin' love,

Lindsay Maxwell

You're a little silly.

And so am I.

And I'll tell you why.

We have this odd tendency to play less than who we are.

You were born from love. You were born from creativity. You were born from truth. You were born to live a beautiful and rich life.

Now, when I say rich, I don't mean money in the bank (though it's always a swell feeling to be able to afford tacos and the occasional scarf).

Your rich life is to be filled with what truly makes your heart sing and others around you sing.

Example:

Have you ever noticed that when you've purchased something you really wanted you enjoy it immensely for days, weeks, months, or even years, but eventually, that novelty does wear off, and you do not place the value in it the same way?

That's because objects and things aren't a sustainable joy. And our feelings transcend and evolve and move forward.

But I will tell you this.

The real goods—the meat and core of life—are found in the simplicity and the peace of it.

You will find sustainable joy in your faith, in your children, in nature, in community, in family, and with friends.

There are walks to be had, volunteering to be done, dinners to cook, wine to pour, tennis to be played . . .

You were born to love. You were born to be free. (And remember, dear friend, freedom doesn't come from running amuck. There are still rules to this playground.)

Oh, you sassy little thing, you were born to engage.

Now go play outside. And don't play any less than that beautiful and shining being that you are.

I can feel your glow,

Lindsay Maxwell

Turn your pain into something beautiful. Turn it into something profound.

It's inevitable, you know. You are going to go through pain. You are going to uncover some scary truths about people. Some of the closest bonds you have with someone can turn on you on a dime. Sometimes without explanation.

And it hurts you to your core. People who have let you down. People who were supposed to be there with you through thick or thin.

Then sometimes life can throw you a curveball. You could be as healthy as an ox, but then the next year you're diagnosed with cancer.

Or your wife leaves you without warning. Or your favorite pet gets hit by a car.

These are all terrible and tragic things. And there is no manual that is given to us about all of these subjects.

Yes, I find solace in the Good Book of the Bible and prayer. Uplifting mentors and philosophers have written and spoken encouragement throughout the ages. You can get some beautiful insight through all of this.

But what do you do with the pain? How do you release it? What are you to make of it?

You turn it into your art. You turn it into something softer, more gentle. You turn it into reading a book or painting a picture or visiting an old friend. You turn it into really listening to other people's stories.

Pain and deep sadness have a way of slowing down time when we are experiencing it. It quiets our mind, and it throws us into being very present in the moment.

I know the suffering.

So I turn it into words. I turn it into phone calls. I turn it into studying my characters. I turn it into a clean and vibrant home. I turn it into muscle mass. I turn it into praying for my foes. I turn it inside out so that none of it will be in vain.

You all have been here on this journey. You have felt your great sorrows and your incredible joys.

What do you do with it?

"Love is something if we give it away . . ."

My encouragement for you is to work through the pain and do something outside of your comfort zone that the pain propelled you to do. Sketch it out. Walk it out. Work it out. Call it out.

Release that.

Love you lots and always,

Lindsay Maxwell

Talk is cheap.

And I love words. Words can ignite the soul and penetrate you on a level that tunes you in.

But words of love, encouragement, promise, and wisdom aren't really meaningful without the intent to follow through. They actually do not emit any energy.

When you encourage, show enthusiasm. When displaying wisdom, talk from experience. When showing love, be present and about the other person. When making a promise, my god, follow through the best you can.

I have called the times we live in the "Instant Gratification Nation."

Everything is at our fingertips, and everything can be treated as disposable. But where is the depth in that? Where is the heart? Where is the meat of the matter?

I encourage and challenge you to let your words land. Have intent with action. Embrace others. Listen.

The world is your oyster. Find the pearl. Look inside.

Love,

Lindsay Maxwell

Your body is a container.

Not only does your body contain all the interesting mass that we are composed of (like bile and stomach acid and bones . . . oh my! [said just like Dorothy in case you didn't get that]), but your body also contains . . . well . . . you!

We are on this planet for our allotted number of years during our journey. We are fortunate enough to hang out in a body while we have our human experience. How neat.

What do you put into your container?

It's the experiences you have, the people you meet, the self-work that you have done, the memories that you keep, and the love that you have within.

And remember, my beautiful friends, we do not want our containers to become too full, burdensome, or heavy.

We need to be constantly adding, eliminating, rejuvenating, and inspiring what we put into our lives.

We are meant to not trudge the heaviness along our journey. Sometimes this is difficult, I know.

My challenge and encouragement for you today is to look inside. What are you putting into your life? What are you afraid to let go of? Do you need to lighten your load? How can you do that to allow more of the sunshine in?

What do you want your life to contain?

Ponder away, you beautiful souls.

Love,

Lindsay Maxwell

Pay attention.

I was blow-drying my hair the other day. And even though I have finer hair, I realized that it was taking forever. I also realized that I was mindlessly blow-drying it while watching Netflix. So I turned off Netflix and started to pay attention to the blow-dryer nozzle and which section of the hair it was hitting. In no time at all, my hair was dry.

Which got me thinking of mindfulness.

So often in life, we want to work toward something—a goal, a test, an audition, a marriage, a fitness level, etc.

Well, we sure can get distracted. We meander around the path to where we want to go (squirrel!), and sometimes we take exceptionally longer to land where we want to.

And that would be okay if we weren't limited for time. But . . . here we are. On this planet for just a blip.

Go out and do it, you guys. Stay aware, stay conscious, stay mindful—stay in the game.

This life is meant to be lived and for you to be connected to people and experiences; feel those feelings—do not Band-Aid them. Seek life and meaning and be fully present while doing so. That's how you slow down time.

You see, time doesn't go by faster as we get older. We are just in our heads more, and when we "wake up," we realize that time just seemed to pass by.

I encourage all of you to take a big stretch, wake up a bit earlier, look at the intricate details in nature, do conscious steps toward a goal, and recognize the value of your minutes.

Doing it all with you as you are not alone,

Lindsay Maxwell

My favorite show to watch is *Wheel of Fortune.*

So naturally, I spent my Saturday night watching it.

For those of you who are not familiar with the game, there is a blank puzzle in a category, and contestants have to spin a wheel and land on a monetary amount and guess a letter, and eventually the letter board fills up, and you solve the puzzle.

Sometimes I can look at the screen and guess it with only a few letters, and I feel like the next Einstein. Other times, I have a blank stare at what one would think is a blatantly obvious answer.

Which got me thinking . . . (You are probably aware by now that I use everyday life experiences as a metaphor for something.)

Sometimes you don't know what you don't know. And once you do know, you cannot "unknow."

We all have our pace in life. Some of us evolve more quickly in some areas, and some take longer than others in certain areas.

One of my favorite quotes from a quirky song from my graduating year called "Everybody's Free to Wear Sunscreen" is this:

"The race is long, and in the end, it's only with yourself . . ."

We are on this planet together for our allotted time slot. We are unwrapping each day as it comes. We are learning, discovering, discarding, recycling, and hoarding our experiences and thoughts with the time we are given.

We are seekers.

My encouragement for you on this fine day is to search out more truth. Do not stop learning. Do not think that you're too old or too set in your way. Yes, you may know a puzzle or two, but you don't know them all right away. Go explore. At your own pace, of course.

I'd like to solve the puzzle, Pat.

Love,

Lindsay Maxwell

"Clear anything in your path that doesn't serve you."

Now, I know that most of you are agreeing with that above statement, and I understand why. When I first saw it as a meme on Instagram, I instantly thought of things, habits, people, and lifestyle norms that I could perhaps clear away.

But then I thought more into it.

It's actually a very self-serving statement.

We think and get caught up with thinking that this life is just all about us—our wants, our needs, our desires. I have coined this era as the "Instant Gratification Nation." And we can be so quick to discard things that no longer "serve us."

We are here on a planet with many personality types and creeds and religions and thought processes. We need to become better at tolerance and patience.

Not everything nor everyone is going to "serve you." But that dynamic still may be necessary.

My encouragement for you today is to really examine what is in your life and the purpose it serves and what you serve to it.

You add value to things that may not add what you deem to be valuable to you.

And that's a gift unto itself.

Love,

Lindsay Maxwell

There is so much good in this world. And there is so much evil.

We live in a world where there are people who give hugs to the brokenhearted. We live in a world where we can go down slides with our children and swing on swings. We live in a world where love blossoms when you least expect it. We live in a world where we get to eat homemade bread and sip on wine from a picnic basket overlooking the Eiffel Tower when we travel.

We also live in a world where unspeakable and unfathomable events happen. We live in uncertainty, mass shootings, illnesses, deaths, starvation, heartaches, and outright selfishness.

This Earth contains all of the good and evil—it always has.

We as humans have such capacity to love and create and live in harmony and in truth.

And we have an innate inclination to destroy, self-serve, and step into darkness.

We are a wee bit messed up, don't you think? And fabulous too.

I am nothing close to perfect, and no one I've ever met is or will be, and I do not expect that from myself nor anyone else, but I will share this with you today:

The closer I am to living in truth and goodness and love (that's what I call God—love), the less frustrated, sad, too absorbed with self, and off purpose I become.

I have been reflecting on what this year held and the other years prior to that. This year contained pretty much every emotion I could think about going through (hey, it only adds to my acting skills to draw upon). What I do know is this:

I have never lived so authentically me and what I'm made from before that. And my life feels more aligned and purpose driven and in tune with love.

My encouragement and challenge for you today is as such: use the brokenness in your life as a pause button. Look deeply into it and see where those wounds truly need to be repaired. Otherwise, you'll always be on repeat.

And you're much too dynamic for that, you sassy thing.

Most of all, though, I'm proud of you and how far you've come in your journey.

Keep going, you little grasshopper.

Love,

Lindsay Maxwell

You are enough.

Yes, you.

You are enough in all your bits and pieces and brokenness and talents and mishaps and quirks.

You are here on Earth for a mere minute in the grand scheme of things. You came into this world like a sponge, and you've soaked up the energy around you. You've dabbled in play, heartache, career, caretaking, monotony, betrayal, loyalty, loss, gains, weight fluctuations, partnerships, and schooling.

Wherever you are in life at this very moment has everything to do with all the moments you have had leading up to now. It's profound and simple at the same time. You're probably just on the couch reading this, and now you're reflecting on all of your moments, and you're like, "Well, here I am . . ."

And that's enough.

You're enough because you're here. You contribute energy and vibration to this ever-evolving (and sometimes unevolving) planet. You give a smile to someone's face. You change diapers. You drive your son to hockey practice. You volunteer at church. You plug somebody's meter. You dry someone's tears.

The little things that you contribute to others are what make this world go round.

My encouragement for you today is to focus on all the good you bring. Stop thinking that you don't bring enough value, worth, or energy to this world. You do. You will continue to. And you're quite dazzling, indeed.

Yes. Dazzling.

With love,

Lindsay Maxwell

Look both ways before you cross the street.

We have all learned that in our early youth, haven't we?

Upon hearing a parent on my street guiding her son crossing the street last week, I, in true Lindsay fashion, applied it to current life; and this is what came to me . . .

When we look both ways before we cross the street, we first look to see if there's someone coming from our left (so we look to the past) or someone coming from our right (our future), and then we quickly look again to our left and then proceed forward.

When we are to make a big decision, we often reflect upon the past and then believe in an unknown future, quickly glance once more behind us, and then take that leap of faith.

The "oncoming" traffic in our road journey will always be there. There are things that will haunt us from our pasts and images that we create about our future that feel daunting.

Your road is full of memories and experiences and will be filled with many more along the way. The truth is, though, is to keep moving. Cross the road. Don't dwell on the past too long and don't fixate on the future.

You don't want to watch life pass you by while you sit and wait for an abandoned and seemingly perfect road.

My encouragement for you today is to take a quick pause to reflect where you have come from and what you've learned and step onto the street and look toward your bright future.

Prance, skip, bunny hop, or strut your way 'cross the road.

Just don't be a chicken.☺

Love,

Lindsay Maxwell

I thought I had lost at love.

Yup. I have had a myriad of relationships throughout the course of my years on Earth. And none have stood the test of time.

While I fully recognize that I am the common denominator with all of my romantic partnerships, don't think it hasn't crossed my mind that I must being doing something out of sorts with the ones whom I have chosen as a partner.

Maybe I have jumped into things too quickly. Maybe I have turned a blind eye to red flags because of my "feelings." Maybe I haven't worked on some key issues that contribute to longevity in a relationship.

Or, as my mama would coin it, maybe I'm just not cut out for a conventional kind of life.

Lord knows I have tried.

For those of you who have been on here for a while, you have seen me through a few dalliances and some more serious encounters.

But . . . I agree with my mama. And it's A-OK.

This blog is written to all you unconventionals out there. I see you. I feel you. I'm with you. Dance your dance. Drum your drum. Flute your flute.

In fact, I have not lost at love, and that is what I want to reiterate. I have found love in the most precious of ways: God first. Family. Friends. Acquaintances. People from different corners of my life.

I have succeeded in love. My self-love is poignant.

My challenge for you this week is to let yourself allow yourself to do it your own way. Find what works for you. There isn't a huge manual. But here we are, thriving and jiving along.

Unconventional looks good on you.

Love,

Lindsay Maxwell

I awoke from a very powerful dream this morning.

In fact, it was so powerful it startled me to wake. And I have to write it out.

In my dream, I was standing in line at the grocery store, and I was picking up a few items for a party I was having at my apartment. I was in party attire, and in front of me there was an extremely frail and elderly woman glancing my way. She looked me up and down, and with a smile and glint in her eyes she said, "Enjoy this time in your life, my dear. It goes by so fast . . ."

Now, I am not a stranger to that kind of wisdom dispensed onto me from the wiser generation, but she then continued, "In the end, it's the funny and what are seemingly insignificant things and memories that get to you. You'll find an old list with your mother's handwritten recipe on it, or a bank receipt from a purchase you made a decade ago. Your childhood home will one day cease to exist, and people from your hometown will forget that you used to climb a certain tree. Time moves so fast, so cherish these moments, and remember all of what I say so that when you get to be my age, you have no regrets and no stone unturned."

I then, in my dream, burst into sobs, knowing sobs. Connected sobs. Not sadness. Not woe. But just the sheer weight and gravity of her words impacted me.

And then I awoke.

I am sentimental.

People matter. Feelings matter. Experiences matter. Love matters. Life matters. Memories matter. It all matters.

This is our one precious, beautiful, messed-up little life. It's weird sometimes, but it's ours.

My encouragement for you today is to make your "now" count. Connect with people. Engage. Enhance. Love like you give a damn.

Understand that it's not meant to be mediocre. You'll often hear me tout that there are things in life to be mediocre about, and love is definitely not one of them.

Joy is in the penmanship of your loved ones. Joy is found in that gentle autumn sunlight on your face. Joy is . . . now.

That's all, folks,

Lindsay Maxwell

Manners never go out of style.

We live in a day and age where we are in go, go, go mode so often. We are busy bees, and that's okay . . . except when we forget our manners.

We all have the same allotted time in our day. We can give a wave to the driver who let us in their lane. We can thank our customers for the nice tip they gave us. We can write thank-you cards for acts of kindness.

I have observed lately that we aren't placing as much importance on our manners. I see people disconnected all too often. I call it the "Instant Gratification Nation."

This blurb is more of a PSA and gentle reminder to us all to slow down.

Let's reach out to one another. Let's be more tolerant and patient. A little thank you can go a long way.

This life is fast. Make an impact. But be kind.

Thanks a bunch for reading,😮

Lindsay Maxwell

I used to love watching DuckTales growing up.

I had a dog named Toto (surprised?), and she would watch it with me. The theme song would come on, and for those who remember, there was a part that went like this:

"DuckTales! Wooooo!"

(Apologies if you get that song stuck in your head.)

Well, I never wanted Toto to feel like ducks were more important, so I would sing along to the theme song and switch "DuckTales" into "DOGtales."

Just to protect her feelings.

So this is my blog today. It's about protecting feelings at the cost of telling people the truth.

In some way or another, we have all covered up, told a white lie, smoothed over the truth, etc.

But why?

We are strong and resilient beings, and even though I probably don't want to know if you like my hair or not, I can handle whatever you throw at me, but only if it's pertinent information.

We tend to gloss over things and make nice and be safe; and if that compromises our truth, authenticity, and values, why do we do it?

It can stem from wanting to be amicable to everyone. It can derive from a lack of self-esteem that comes with a "people pleasing" nature.

I have had jabs, stabs, offside insults, and downright rude comments thrown at me throughout my life. It's part and parcel of being in the public eye.

But guess what? I survived. And I realize that people operate from where their life and mindsets are.

Kind, content, joyous, and stable people don't go looking for the negative. They just don't. What you seek, you shall find.

My encouragement and challenge for you today is to be real with yourself first. And, in turn, be real with those around you. Sing "DuckTales!"

Just don't let Toto hear it. I don't think she's ready yet.☺

Love your faces and all your bits,

Lindsay Maxwell

I used to hate country music.

In fact, it made me shudder.

I have since changed.

While I am still not a huge fan of the twang, I found truth in the lyrics. Real and raw truth.

So it got me thinking as I tend to think about everything my days offer, and I thought about how we are living our lives.

Are you living in truth? How do you know if you are? What is your truth?

You see, in exchange for one day of your life, you are given an opportunity to develop yourself. You can use that gift to enhance, learn a new trick, mend a relationship, or read until your heart's content.

What I know is that we are here on this planet for an allotted amount of time. There is only one me, and there is only one you. You do not have to be a facsimile of someone else's wants and ideals of you.

You offer a unique gift and a certain spice to life. Your essence has a presence that you impose onto each person.

In fact, you're a little dash of magic just as you are.

My encouragement for you today is to step into your truth. Are you living your most authentic life? Are you honoring your instincts and intuition? Are you being honest with others about what you desire from them?

This is our one whimsy of a life, dear friend.

Go get 'em, partner.

(Spoken like a true cowgirl.)

Love,

Lindsay Maxwell

Don't be a short bloom.

So often in life, we get excited about new adventures; and we put our energy, thoughts, passion, and investments into it: relationships, careers, friendships, and education.

While all of that beautiful emotion is fragrant, full of life, and effervescent, it is not sustaining enough to hold on to all of the above.

I have observed a lot in my time here. I have seen quick dalliances. (I love you. Now I don't.) I have seen people swinging from vine to vine in careers. (Try this new flavor of the month.) I have seen high turnovers of friendships. (Ooh, a hundred pennies vs. four quarters! Squirrel!). And I have observed people rushing through their education. (Are we there yet?)

If you wish to sustain and "bloom," it is best to be consistent, mindful, aware, and intentional. We are not designed to merely flit and flutter our way through life. There wouldn't be any solid ground for us to have the sustaining roots.

This is not a surface life. This is our big story. Make your chapters count. Make your words have meaning.

My challenge and encouragement for you today is to take a look at some of the areas in your life and see where you can water, nurture, and feed. See where you need to tend to—with mindfulness and care.

Don't wilt past your prime.

Love you,

Lindsay Maxwell

One person's junk is another person's treasure.

I was walking around my neighborhood the other day, and my head was down, and I wasn't really taking in my surroundings; I mean, I see that same view almost every day. And as much as I love my hood, I am not always in awe every moment with buildings, sidewalks, etc.

I looked at a bank building that isn't the one that I personally deal with, and I had an "aha!" moment.

What is humdrum and insignificant to me could be a beacon for someone else.

Maybe that bank is a lifesaver for a person who needs exactly that one in that moment.

A person with fresh eyes on that street may perceive those buildings differently. They may appreciate the intricate architecture or placement of brick.

You see, we are human. No matter where we are, who we are with, what we drive, the clothes we wear, we eventually get more familiar with it; and sometimes (and this is where the blog gets real) we become a little blind to life and others.

We then want to explore new neighborhoods, new people, new clothes, new destinations, and (sometimes) a new partner.

Okay. Yes. We are curious by nature, and we are ever expanding.

But there's a healthy balance between "chasing the dragon" and being content in your own backyard.

My encouragement for you (as I have been experimenting with this for some time now) is to write down a list of things that you are grateful for. Start with ten things. Even do it on your phone.

Then write down ten things you want to change or enhance.

You are given this life. You are going to have moments of desires and content.

Again . . . human.

Just don't forget the trimmings, filling, and all that good stuff in between.

Love,

Lindsay Maxwell

You did not sign up for a life of mediocracy.

No, I am not saying that if you are not doing crazy and death-defying stunts you're not living a full life. It's not about that.

It is about putting weight, purpose, intention, love, and legacy into your days.

You are here, and you are now.

You have awakened into this new day, and the week is before you. Why not mindfully interact with those around you and the sights that you see and the people you come across?

If you've been reading my blogs for some time, you will notice an underlying message in each of them . . .

We are limited for time, and you are much more of a brilliance than you could ever comprehend in yourself.

You need not to play less than what you are designed.

And you are gently flowing along in this life—along with bumps, hurdles, kisses, heart beams, and slivers intertwined.

Your life is not linear. You go forward and backward and sideways and topsy-turvy.

But it is yours. And it is anything but mediocre.

There are a lot of people on this planet. Each one of you contains a myriad and range of emotions/feelings/personalities/hormones/gifts.

Those are a lot of ingredients. You are the whole darn cookbook!

My encouragement for you today is to be kind to yourself and recognize that at any given moment, life can change. You aren't your past. Your future is always shifting and available . . . until it's not. So go forth and seek.

Your world is waiting.

Love you,

Lindsay Maxwell

How is this chapter in your life going?

You see, your life is a grand book. It's filled with chapters that make absolutely nonsequential . . . sense.

If you were the reader of your life, I'll bet you that you could read the whole thing; and with all those plot twists, topsy-turvies, jolts, mundaneness, exhilarations, and conversations written in your story, you'd be likely to scratch your head and wonder, "What the heck did I just read?"

Your story isn't linear.

Neither is mine.

It doesn't work that way.

Nor should it.

We tend to think that we are our own author, but can you truly say with total certainty that everything you have ever mapped out turned out just the way you planned?

I mean, what's the fun in that?

The golden treasure is hidden in the unknown. As you unfold each page, you enter a new day. And each new day brings upon us a new week, month, year, decade, etc.

My encouragement for you today is to enjoy the words that fill up each page. Do not expect it to be a book filled with the same paragraph over and over.

You're a good read.

With love,

Lindsay Maxwell

Don't skim your way through life.

Oftentimes, we have a tendency to skim through the "boring times" in life to get to the goods. We are half asleep just going through life so that we can get to the weekend, the next vacation, the favorite TV show, your nap time, to when you fall in love, your graduation, etc.

Those are all exciting things and experiences (especially that nap time), but there are far more moments in between than there are just in those grandiose moments.

And if we were to just skim and skimp over those moments in between, why, it would kind of almost be just like a leap year day now, wouldn't it?

An event that only happens once every so often.

But it's those moments in between, those quiet coffee moments, those reflective moments, those getting-ready-for-work-and-doing-up-your-watch moments—those are the silly, nonimportant moments that add up to our time spent here on Earth.

My encouragement for you today is to pay attention. This is our one little life. There are treasures and riches to be had in those passerby moments.

Tie those shoelaces with pride!

Love you,

Lindsay Maxwell

It's scary not knowing the answer, isn't it? And it's even scarier not knowing the future.

However, when in life have we ever known for certain what our tomorrows held for us?

Yes, our tomorrows came with a sense of routine. We can agree upon that.

We trusted in our jobs being there. We trusted in our schools and classes carrying on as normal, and we knew that on the weekend, we could make plans at a restaurant and eat there. All seemingly mundane but dependable scenarios.

And now we are left with a sense of uncertainty.

One of my acting mentors often spoke about being and living in the moment. That we cannot suddenly travel back in time nor hop on a bus to our unknown future.

All we have is now.

Our now has always been uncertain, always not a guarantee.

Being human is full of uncertainty and twists and turns.

This is a pretty darn large plot twist, isn't it?

But life will continue on, and we will move through this, and things will be different on the other side. And we don't know what that looks like at the moment.

We never really had a crystal ball, my friends. We had routines and expectations and security, but this life is a strange little ditty, isn't it?

My gentle encouragement for you today is to fully engage in your moments. Watch your children play. Submerse yourself in that book.

Chop up those veggies at dinner and notice the seeds in the green peppers or the rich red colors in your tomato.

We are in this together. We can use it to worry about "what's next," or we can use it to engage in "what's now."

There are many apexes and exhilarating speeds on this roller coaster of life. Have faith. We are never alone.

Love,

Lindsay Maxwell

Dolce far niente.

The sweetness of doing nothing.

I don't know about you, but we seem to have a lot of that more often. Or a lot of that as an option that wasn't so readily present before.

I used to feel extreme guilt if I wasn't using my minutes and hours and days to create or produce something. I wanted to prove to myself that the days I was given weren't just wasted or in vain.

Until I burned myself out.

This burnout landed a few years ago; and so I packed my bags, booked a ticket, brought two books and my journal, and took myself to a resort for five days in Palm Springs.

I admit, it took me a couple of nights to fully submerse myself in traveling alone. I mean, I wasn't *that* far away from home, but this was my first time hopping on a plane to go to a place that wasn't for work or a trip with friends or a significant other.

Then it hit me. That sweetness of doing nothing.

I was in the pool on a blow-up floaty with a glass of lime fizzy water in hand. It was 10:00 a.m. There wasn't a cloud in the sky. There was the most gentle breeze that caused the palm trees in the distance to sway. There was low-volume resort music playing classic hits in the background. And I thought to myself in that quiet, yet so poignant, moment, *This is it. There's nothing I have to do, feel, give, receive, or be . . .*

I lay there like a sloth (mind you, a very content sloth) and lazily floated around having not a care in the world.

But I knew myself. I knew that once I returned home, I would feel a sense of obligation, maybe remorse, maybe too much self-pressure.

So I vowed that I would put in my luggage that feeling. That peaceful joy of the sweetness of doing nothing. And never would I feel guilty again for taking that time in increments to myself.

My friends, we are all experiencing our own perceptions to this collective experience. There is a lot of fear and woe, rightly so.

I am here to remind you (and myself) that if there is a part of you that is feeling like you're not being enough with this extra time upon you, I encourage you to slip away in your mind for a bit because there truly is a little treasure in *dolce far niente.* The sweetness of doing nothing.

Be well.

Love,

Lindsay Maxwell

I saw the leaves rustling in the wind the other day.

The wind carried on as the leaves on the branches swayed to and fro.

The trees didn't know that there was currently a worldwide pandemic occurring. (Or maybe they do as trees can be very sensitive.) The trees and wind just carried about in their own fashion.

It gave me comfort.

We, as human beings, enjoy both sides of the coin. We love spontaneity, and we also love having sense of predictability as well. Nothing is wrong with either.

Times like these, however, propel us into the unknown and uncertainty, but we are always in that. This is just a different scale.

This life that we are currently all living in for our allotted time provides us with ups, downs, backwards, forwards, and sometimes topsy-turvies.

Your leaves will rustle, yes. But the tree that you are stands firm and rooted.

My encouragement for you this week is to perhaps journal about this interesting time in our lives. Set aside ten to fifteen minutes and have a real check-in or record where you're at. This too shall pass.

Smiling at you from here,

Lindsay Maxwell

We are doomed.

Okay. Okay. A little dramatic and morbid for a Sunday morning, I know. However, we are doomed, but not in the way you think.

We are doomed to the inevitable phenomenon of what I like to call "growth."

You see, we as humans are always reforming, changing, obtaining, releasing, engaging, and experiencing. We go through our days, weeks, months, and years transitioning in every way, sometimes at a minute scale and sometimes not.

You are not the same person you were in the tenth grade. You are not the same person that you were last year.

You may have the same essence, yes, but you now have new tools and gadgets in your belt.

You are allowed to allow yourself to respond differently than you used to. You have learned so much in your given time, and that is a gift. What you may have thought was an impossible task to confront before, you may be able to tackle it head-on now.

Because . . . you are doomed.

Doomed to the fate of growth and change and perseverance. Doomed to the whim of time. Doomed to having the right to excel and enhance. Doomed to step into your beautiful birthright of greatness.

My encouragement for you today is to reflect upon where you have observed areas in your life where you have grown and faced some fears that the old you wouldn't have had the gumption to. We all have triumphs and tribulations. It's good to remember what you've overcome to get you to where you are now.

I think you're swell.

Love,

Lindsay Maxwell

Turn your face toward the sun.

The truth of the matter is that what you seek, you will always—and I mean always—find.

If you are naturally inclined to look for the negative in people, by gum, you'll find it.

If you love to perpetuate terrible news and relive the same situation where you were wronged in the past, by golly, you will perpetuate even more of that.

However, if you start to realize that a tremendous amount of your little yet profound experience on this imperfect planet has an inkling to do with your perceptions and the way you process things (and, dear reader, I am not blind to the notions and facts that some of us are dealt a lot of bad hands that mar us from being able to process things as simply as "facing the sun"; sigh, utmost respect to your journey), then I humbly suggest you start from within and dig to find instances, people, experiences, memories, etc., in which you are grateful for.

Look, we are truly here for a shimmer of time. Yes, I know we live in the moment, and some of us have had a longer time to have moments than others.

I am no stranger to moments in which I wish did not happen.

However, I still look toward brighter days.

Because, well, it feels good.

I am going to leave you on a different note today. A quote written by F. Scott Fitzgerald:

"For what it's worth . . . it's never too late, or in my case too early, to be whoever you want to be. There's no time limit. Start whenever you want. You can change or stay the same. There are no rules to this thing.

We can make the best or the worst of it. I hope you make the best of it. I hope you see things that startle you. I hope you feel things you never felt before. I hope you meet people who have a different point of view. I hope you live a life you're proud of, and if you're not, I hope you have the courage to start all over again."

Love,

Lindsay Maxwell

Have you done it yet?

I do not know what your particular "it" is, but I want to know if you've done it.

And if not, why not?

It could be starting a task, cleaning your garage, making amends with your parent, apologizing for a wrongdoing, learning a few new words in another language, starting the gym, and my list can go on and on.

There are a lot of "its" in this world. There are a plethora of opportunities (and obstacles, I know).

However, as mentioned in previous blogs, we are allotted only a certain amount of time on this wee planet of ours. You have purpose. You have tasks. You have adventures and to do's.

Nike has this little slogan: Just Do It.

I think they were on to something.

Now, now. I understand perfectly that there are certain circumstances that may temporarily stunt our "its" currently.

My gentle guidance and encouragement for you is to make a list of little things you can do right now to work toward accomplishment.

It feels good to finish it.

Just try not to look like Cousin It.

Love,

Lindsay Maxwell

I stared at a rock for a solid five minutes the other day.

No, I am not off doing peyote or ayahuasca in the middle of the desert. However, that particular rock taught me a lot in those precious five minutes.

It was a large rock, almost a boulder. It had mossy overgrowth on it. It would be too large to manually move.

And . . . it's going to be in that same exact spot long after you and I are gone. And . . . it won't care (if rocks were to have feelings).

You see, other than having a staring contest with said rock, I was also privy to the birds flapping around, the trees swaying back and forth with the rustling of the gentle wind, and the creek babbling over to and fro.

This made me realize, in my coffee stupor, just how insignificant *and* significant life and problems and circumstances are.

They are insignificant to the birds, to nature, and to Old Father Time. Yet they are so significant to us and our journey and our moments.

The show goes on, though. Time does not stop. Things carry on. We all have a purpose and a mission to carry out; be it grandiose or not, we still have one.

My wee encouragement for you today is to slow down a bit. Yes, it's easy to get caught up in life's woes and woos. Remember, my dear friend, that the sun will rise and the sun will set each day. And each day offers up a supply of nourishment, whimsies, laughs, stubbed toes, a few bathroom visits, and (if you're lucky) a couple of viewed shooting stars here and there.

Life is meant to be lived and respected.

PS. I totally won that staring contest.

Love,

Lindsay Maxwell

I was lying in bed the other night, and a thought came into my head. I thought to myself, *I am now one day closer to my last day on Earth . . .*

I promise, I am not morbid or constantly thinking about my time. However, those little thoughts do come in, and I let them. Because it's reality. We are all given an allotted number of days, and it's what we do with them that counts.

I know. It gives me anxiety as well.

But . . . it also brings me to this topic:

If you look at your life on a sheet of paper and there's a start and stop date, I bet you would want to fill the in-betweens with really cool stuff. Right?

We do not know when our end date is. We do not know when our friends' and loved ones' end dates are. What I do know, though, is that I do not want to spend a day that is such a gift doing mundane and nonproductive things. And by productive, I don't just mean work. You can be productive by expanding your mind by reading or attending a class. I believe in growing at any age.

Don't limit yourself. I find that we can become too complacent in our current situations.

I love what Tony Robbins said once, "You will tolerate it until you can't tolerate it anymore."

Well, guess what? I cannot tolerate knowing that I have an expiry date on Earth and letting my precious life pass. Our time is valuable. I challenge you to ask yourself this question:

"What do I want to fill my 'in-between' days up with?"

Do you want to repeat the same years over and over again? Nah! Even if you are at 100 percent right now, there will be always room to grow and learn. That's the way the movement of life is. Forward. Not backward.

You are not your past. You are not that awkward teenager. You are not the outcast. You belong with this beautiful universe. You are a child of it. You are the copilot—that's a pretty big deal.

I believe in you. I believe in myself. And I believe in us as a collective community. Let us step into our roles of becoming better; it's a bit-by-bit process. Small steps and the journey.

You know what? There *will* be bumps and bruises along the way. There *will* be moments of self-doubt. There *will* be triumphs and accomplishments. There *will* be all of it!

Looks like you're filling up your "in-between" with an awesome pulse instead of a dull flatline, though.

Clear,

Lindsay Maxwell

I have contracted a fear of heights.

It developed a few years ago, and it irks me.

However, I loathe the sensation of going up in planes, bridges, and escalators even.

So in essence, I have a fear of ascension.

Going down = no problem.

Maybe it's because I'm a Virgo and that means I'm an earth sign so I like to be grounded? Who knows?

However, it irks me even more that my fear has stunted me from certain things.

I am at a point in my life where I am reflecting on what I have done for the past fifteen years (so many of my dreams have come into fruition), but I am a feisty lass, and I like a good ol' challenge every now and then.

I am going to add another tool to my tool belt in the near future. But change, like heights, scares me. It plays into my anxious side.

So in order for me to confront fear, I need to put it into a physical action.

I went on a walk the other day. I usually do the same routine (which is a beautiful walk by the seawall). As I was headed toward there, I saw a bridge in front of me, one that I have driven over many times. I even attempted to walk over that bridge a few years back and had to turn around in fear of me getting an anxiety attack, and having that sensation paralyzes me.

But that day, I decided that I would cross that bridge, even if it meant feeling uncomfortable. Even if I had an anxiety attack. Even if I hated every minute of it.

So I approached that bridge, and tears sprung into my eyes.

I crossed it.

I told myself that if I'm to venture into unknown and new territory, I have to *feel* it in my physical body.

Because we are mind, body, and soul, you know.

I saw angles and terrain and views from that bridge had I never walked it and only driven. I got my steps in.

But most of all, I confronted my fear.

Now I know I can do anything.

Well, within reason.

My encouragement for you this week is to feel that fear and do it anyway. Seriously. Do it. It's less daunting than you think.

Shimmy that fanny of yours, you daredevil, you.

Love,

Lindsay Maxwell

It's over between us.

This whole living-in-the-past thing? It's sooooo early 2000s.

You are not bound by anything you have experienced prior to right now.

That is the sheer beauty of our moments, hours, days, and weeks.

We are constantly given fresh time, particles, temperatures, movements, and chances each and every day.

We know this in theory, yes. We may even catch glimpses of anew. But how do we practice being present with our current rather than dwelling on the past?

Discipline.

Ugh. I shudder at that word too.

When you go into your memory bubble and start to dwell on past defeats, woes, patterns, or habits, do something mindful and intentional to bring you back into present time, for that is where true creation happens.

My encouragement for you this week is to make baby steps toward shedding some skin that no longer serves you nor others and step into this very pulsating moment and take on all that encompasses it.

You'll live longer. Trust me.

I have all the faith in you.

Love,

Lindsay Maxwell

Stop being a slave to others.

You see, we go through this life with a hope that most people think the way we do, that they have the same feelings, thoughts, desires, processes, empathy, and compassion.

News flash!

They don't. So don't waste your time nor energy expecting that they will match you. And that's okay.

People have their own sets of beliefs, systems, viewpoints, hardwiring, and ingrained programming as their filter on how they see and perceive you.

We give so much attention to the way we are received that we sometimes lose ourselves and our authenticity in the vanity of pleasing others. And why? So that we will have the approval of someone who doesn't *really* see us at our core?

This is your beautiful life, and each one of you has a special gift to give. Your gift is different than my gift, and each one is so valuable.

I know we are human. I know we like to people please at times and live up to a certain expectation of others. It's a part of our experience while here on Earth.

But in that mix, don't forget to offer up what nobody else has: *you!*

My encouragement for you this week is to unapologetically operate from your true form. Be comfortable (or uncomfortable) in the state of just being you.

You are lovely just as you are. No need for approval.

Keep that chin up, boys and gals.

Love,

Lindsay Maxwell

You really don't need to hide.

In fact, it's quite lovely when you come out and play.

Each one of us has every possible emotion somewhere within us. We all have the capacity to feel love, anger, happiness, despair, rage, loneliness, joy, and every other color of the rainbow. It's woven into our comprised spirit, and it's there for us to access at any time.

Events and circumstances can bring them to surface. These emotions and feelings can be triggered into existence.

It's absolutely impossible and would be kind of odd, to say the least, to reside in a state of "everything is fine" all of the time.

Because . . . sometimes everything is not fine. And yet we try to portray that it is.

We do that out of fear of being judged. We don't want to be deemed as "too much" or "too overwhelming," and, heaven forbid, "too dramatic."

We are all subjected to the possible pleasantries and possible horrors that this human experience can offer us. Nobody is exempt.

This life can offer us dear friends, delicious cake, seeing new sights in a different country, falling in love, watching your child learn to share, and little everyday joys.

This same life can offer us cancer, insufficient funds, inexplicable cruelty, deterioration of what you thought was a solid relationship, loss of a family member, and everyday waves of sadness.

The truth is that we all have it within. We are not alone with our load of joys and sorrows.

No need to hide them from others. We all got 'em too. In fact, you help people along their journey by sharing. It accelerates the process and assists them by "unstucking" themselves.

My encouragement for you this week is to allow yourself to sit with your current state of emotions. Maybe even say a hello to them. Get to know them. Share your thoughts with a friend. Stop playing "hide-and-go-seek."

Shed some light on your dark.

Bring your brilliance forward.

Love,

Lindsay Maxwell

Life is not for the faint of heart.

And sometimes, my friends, we have faint hearts.

Over the past few months, years, heck, span of my lifetime thus far, I have had many tumultuous experiences—many profound, many uplifting, and a few gut wrenchingly heart crushing.

My writing may resonate with some of you. It may repel some of you. It may make some of you a little curious. And it may even open some of you.

You all have heard the saying "Jesus saves."

Well, as amazing and ineffable that statement is for me, yesterday I had an even more eye-opening imprint on my heart:

"Jesus keeps saving . . ."

I was having a good old gusher of a soul cry. I was releasing a lot of pent-up emotions that I have been avoiding to touch on for some time. (It feels good to do from time to time. Highly recommended.)

I was Rudolph the Red-Nosed Reindeer's deranged-looking twin: red nose, puffy eyes, blotchy skin, and I tell ya . . . I wasn't cute.

So . . . I started to pray. I just prayed for peace and understanding, and I prayed to let go of me trying to "fix it" in my head.

I truly felt the presence of God, and he said, "Lindsay, you beautiful little mess, let me handle this." (Okay . . . I threw in the beautiful part, but it sounds like something he would say.)

As soon as I felt those words, I experienced a bathtub-temperature peace engulf me. I also felt as though I lost twelve pounds.

He showed up. Again. And again. And always will.

You all know I rarely talk religion or politics on here. It's not something I'm here to do. And I don't even consider myself religious. I love God with all of me, but I am *farrrrrrr* from being a "perfect Christian."

I will tell you this, though. I felt it. I feel it now. And I will continue to feel it. My testimony is such.

My encouragement for you all this week is to relish in the fact that no matter what your spiritual belief is, you are loved. You're made from love. You come from love. You *are* love. And it never fails.

You'll see.

Keep it up,

Lindsay Maxwell

I am a villain.

Yup. In someone's story out there, I'm their villain. And in someone else's story, so are you.

We are also a hero.

We are also a mystery.

We are perceptions of the inner workings of people's minds—the impacts we have made, the deeds we have done, and the words we have said.

And from their perspective, we are seen through the eyes and heart of their own experiences and processes through life.

In my younger years, I used to place too much weight on how people perceived me and if they liked what I presented.

I have learned not too long ago (and what a valuable lesson, indeed) that it is positively silly to place so much importance on what people thought or felt about me.

We do our best. We help others. We love the way we know how, we grow, we falter at times, we say and do things that can be really messed up, and we reach the end of day with a reflection.

We are all very similar yet extremely unique.

My challenge and encouragement for you this week is to start operating from a truly authentic place. Don't pay too much mind on others' perceptions of you. Do you.

For what it's worth, though . . .

I think you're grand.

Love,

Lindsay Maxwell

What are we so afraid of?

I was sitting at a coffee shop and doing a little experiment last week. I purposely positioned myself at a table by the window to watch people passing by. I had my phone tucked away (a true rarity) and just sat there and observed people walking by while sipping on my coffee. It was late afternoon, and the sun was gently starting to set.

Now, just to paint you a picture, I wasn't *staring* at the passersby, but I would glance at them as they walked by and give a slight smile or nod, but my energy and demeanor wasn't invasive or intrusive. Or weird (I hope).

The results are in. Drumroll . . .

People are uncomfortable with making eye contact and wary of smiling at strangers!

They would catch my eye and immediately grab their phone, fake cough (that's my favorite along with the fake sniffle), or just look down at their shoes.

I mean, I'm not an intimidating-looking lass. I don't look like I could harm you (though I have been going hard at the gym, so watch it). But not one person smiled back or locked eyes with me.

We are all busy and on the move, I know. But eye contact and acknowledgment are still a form of subtle communication.

Do we need to slow down? Do we need to start seeing people? Are we losing our innate nature of being able to exchange energy with a stranger?

I love to connect. That's my heartstring. I can feel people as soon as they walk into a room. I can feel them through the written word. I can feel loved ones when they're miles away. Energy is emitted at all times, and it doesn't have physical boundaries.

I then wondered if for some reason there was a catastrophe and there were only a few hundred human beings left in our area, would we be eternally grateful to see a new face, feel a new soul, and make a connection?

What I want to challenge and encourage you for this week is to be more aware of your surroundings and people whom you pass. Even if you're not a people person, strike up a conversation with a stranger. Smile at your neighbor. Give a compliment to your barista. Engage. Connect.

I am a part of all that I have met. (Alfred, Lord Tennyson)

I think you're cute,

Lindsay Maxwell

People are going to do really messed-up things to you in life.

People will scorn you, laugh at you, abandon you, and bring you down. It is a very sad but very truthful fact.

Well, now that we've exposed that lovely nugget of information, I'll let you in on a little secret. It is how you respond to these people that will lead you to the life you want to live.

You cannot control others in behavior, thoughts, actions, or intentions. People, at some point in your life, are going to do what they're going to do regardless of how you feel about it. Or the impact it will have on you.

We have all hurt people whether it be unintentionally or intentionally.

I'm sure, as you are human, that you have.

And you've had it done to you. And that's the not-so-pleasant part of this game of life.

But are we here to simply throw ourselves into a category of just "being human," or shall we live with the intention that we are divine and here on the physical plane just for a mere blip?

I observe human behavior quite often. I'm in touch with emotion as my chosen (well, it actually chose me) profession is expressing all the nitty-gritty feelings that come into my vessel. Whether it's from someone else's written words or my own experiences, I observe and feel and then act accordingly.

What I see in this era that we live in is what I have coined as the "Instant Gratification Nation."

Oh, I'm guilty as sin for some of what I'm about to point out, so don't you think I'm getting away scot-free.

We want something, we buy it. Even if it goes on the credit card.

We *fall out of love* with our spouse . . . well, let's just throw in the towel after a year of marriage.

We don't see results at the gym? Meh, might as well just quit.

It is this self-serving and self-seeking attitude that gives us a sensation that we will only be happy with the "what's next."

We are the only generation that does not place value on the simple and beautiful things as our ancestors did. So much is at our fingertips and can be replaced that there is a sense of important things, people, and experiences that lack the real value to us.

What is sacred to you? What is irreplaceable?

My challenge and encouragement for you this week is to get to the root of your heart. Ask yourself what matters? Who matters? What can you do for others that brings beauty and richness and deep value to their lives? Try not to self-indulge too much. Give.

With all the gentle nudges,

Lindsay Maxwell

I had a pedicure the other day.

The woman accidentally cut my foot while she was using the pumice scrub on my feet. It's about the size of a large paper cut, and it stung like hell. That being said, it was one of the best pedicure experiences I had ever had. She gave me three massages: oil, citrus scrub, and lotion.

I was sitting there (in the massage chair, nonetheless) in total bliss except when I would get the occasional stinging sensation from the cut.

It made me reflect on life (of course . . . because life is happening all around us, and we are here to observe and engage).

I was thinking about the human psyche and how our attention can so easily go to the painful thoughts or the irksome thoughts so easily and even when everything else in life is going just dandy.

It's the same as when ten people could give you a compliment but that one person could say something offside and *that's* where you put your focus on.

Why do we do that!

I'll tell you why.

Brace yourself.

Because . . . our spirit is made from harmony, creativity, joy, love, flow, and magnificence. When we are in our stride, that's our natural state. When something "goes against the grain," it cuts us because it feels unnatural to us and our state of innate being.

So the next time you have a fickle friend, pay no mind. Think of all the other amazing friends you have. The next time an upset happens at work, think about all the value you bring to the table. The next time you suffer from a breakup, remember that your heart is leading you to something even more suited for you.

Our focus and attention are important tools for this game we are experiencing in life. Remember that, my beautiful friends.

With a Band-Aid on my big toe,

Lindsay Maxwell

I still watch cartoons. I still play video games, and I still sort of believe in Santa Claus.

And I am in my forties.

I know that we each have our "grand entrances" and our "grand exits," and some "exits" happen much sooner than we or our loved ones could ever predict.

Which is what this blog is innately about.

Your time.

"Growing older is a privilege denied to many . . ."

I don't know about you, but I have loved pretty much every year of my life thus far. That doesn't go without saying that I haven't had moments of despair, heartache, trials, embarrassments, mistakes, and wrongdoings. Nope, I've had all of those and some unmentionables.

But . . . as I look back on my life and I see it in colors, I see brightness on my grand mural. I see rich shades and only minor dark contrasts. It makes for a fabulous painting. And it's so not done.

My time here will one day cease to be. So while I'm here, I'm really committed to "being here."

What does that mean? What does that look like?

Well, I'm going to show up and confront. I'm going to go after my dreams. I'm going to connect with people, forgive easily, express, eat, give even when I feel like I'm in a lack (because no matter what your bank account says, my friends, you should always give what you can to help, and it doesn't just have to be monetary).

Why waste any precious and delicious time we have here? We have all lost dear friends, family, and colleagues to their "exits."

We need to live while we are here. This is our time.

Look, I don't always live my life all zen'd out and in the state of eternal bliss—impossible and unrealistic. And kind of weird. But I do place *value* on this experience.

We were given a body (neat!), and we are a soul. And we have our individual personalities. And we have food. And we have music. And we have carnivals and celebrations and Christmas trees and goats!

There it is, boys and girls, we have a lot. And we are a lot. We are complex and intricate creatures.

But our time is now.

Hint: Try not to let it pass you by.

With a wee nudge,

Lindsay Maxwell

You have failed.

Yes, you have failed miserably at giving up. Because look at you, you are alive today. You've shown up to today; and you are breathing, reading, feeling, and living.

That grand failure of yours has brought you to a magnificent time in your life. The *right now.*

What, are you waiting until next week for your life to be magnificent? Are you waiting until Christmas so that things will magically turn themselves around? Next spring?

Ah no, my beautiful friends. The magic of life happens in the now. This is it. All that you've ever done leading up to this day—the good, the bad, and the ugly—has led you to this: Now. Here. Hi.

Today is the day you can start at the gym. Today is the day that you can call that friend you haven't spoken with in years. Today is the day you can leave that toxic relationship. Today is the day you can purchase that ticket to the moon.

"There is no time like the present."

"If not now, then when?"

We've heard those before.

Sit with these words this morning. Really look at your life. Are you living in the now? Or are you living to lead up to an unknown future? Plan and prepare, of course, but don't forget that this . . . is it. And it is good.

I'm glad you failed at giving up so that you could be here today to sit with me and have a visit.

Cheers to that lovely heart of yours that beats so eloquently now,

Lindsay Maxwell

I am sorry to tell you this, but you need to lose weight . . .

Oh, come on, do you really think I'm talking about your body weight? Nope.

You need to lose the weight you carry from yesterday and all the days before that.

Has it ever serviced you to bring your past problems into today's present?

I can assure you that it has not.

Each day brings a new life to your world. You are allowed to start fresh, and you are allowed to release what no longer serves you where it belongs—in the past.

The past is there to remind us of what we want for our future and what we do not want. It's an entity to reflect upon for mere seconds to guide us but not to stay in.

It's actual insanity the amount of hurts, upsets, disappointments, and tribulations we carry into a day that holds triumphs, joys, love, forgiveness, and romance.

Do not deny yourself the riches that a new day provides. Be here now. You cannot physically transport back or forward in time, and even if you could, you'd be there now. (How's that for an early morning mind trip?)

Rascals, go and live. It's a privileged denied to so many. It's a beautiful and life-giving day out there.

You're not your yesterday. You're not your October 27, 2001.

You are not even your five minutes ago . . .

Shed that weight. It's not yours to carry anymore. The past had it all sorted.

With love and a little bit of dazzle,

Lindsay Maxwell

Don't kill the magic.

Did you know that certain areas of our lives hold a certain amount of magic within them? Areas such as relationships, playtime, learning, and solace?

Let me elaborate.

Relationships are a tricky one, aren't they? We get into them, and we feel all those heightened feelings of euphoria, connection, elevation, and twitterpation. We cannot imagine not feeling those feelings for our significant other. The passion, the razzle-dazzle . . . my god, there is nothing like it, is there?

But . . . along the way, a certain critter creeps in. We will call him "Expectation." Expectation kills the magic in all things. We start to expect our partners to provide things for us that no person should place on another person. Things like fulfilling our ego, our ideal of how we "should" be treated. And yes, to a certain extent, we should expect something. But it's when we get the complacent expectation and stop putting into the coin jar of relationships that it eventually runs out and dries up. How dull, right?

The age-old question is how to keep that magic alive? I feel like I know it in theory; don't stop courting your significant other, live in the moment with presence, take individual time for yourselves, and don't expect them to be your everything all the time.

Human beings are complex. We are a lot of work and mechanisms and idiosyncrasies. No two relationships are alike, but when you feel the magic, it's important to keep it alive. Water that shit. Make it grow.

There are few things in life that heighten us like relationships do. So why treat it like it's mediocre? Almost laughable, isn't it?

The true magic in life, though, comes from you. Your infinite ability to create, succeed, overcome, and power through. You were woven out of love, and all that is phenomenal.

Whyever play less than that? This world is your playground to seek out and explore. There is magic in knowing the power and delight that dwells within you.

As I write to you, some of you will totally connect and agree with what I'm affirming, and some of you aren't on that path or maybe don't want to be. All good. I want to express to all you gorgeous souls that you're stronger than you'll ever know. You are more competent than you can comprehend. And you are a brilliance.

You *are* the magic. Don't kill it by forgetting that. It goes where you go. Travel lightly.

Enjoy,

Lindsay Maxwell

You're not here to work, pay bills, and die.

Break that cycle if that's the path you're on or in danger of becoming on.

Yes, having money in the bank is wonderful. It affords us to live our lifestyles. Yes, being debt free is a better option than owing creditors money because it makes you feel responsible and free. And yes, having an overflow of abundance feels extraordinary because you can buy what you wish, travel where you want, and freely give without noticing it missing from your wallet too much.

Money is energy—just like everything else in life. It flows to us and from us and is used for many means. However, it's how your inner dialogue and relationship with money that determines the majority of where your current finances are at.

But I'm not here to talk solely about money today. I'm here to talk about your simple pleasures that don't cost a darn thing.

When the stress of finances weighs in your heart and head, it's so easy to forget the wonders and lusters that surround you. That's why it's vital to still live a rich life even if your bank account doesn't reflect.

And, disclaimer, you can still do that while being a hard worker. It's about prioritizing your mind, body, and soul.

If you're in a relationship, please (for the love of God) do not stop courting your spouse due to the everyday monotony. It will kill your passion. Instead, set a time to unplug from social media, emails, etc., and go for a walk or cook a meal together, or visit an art museum. Hold hands. Kiss. Ask them questions. Even if you've been together a hundred years. Heck, tickle each other until you're pink in the face. I don't care what you do. Keep fanning that spark. You'll thank me later.

If all you do is work, work, work, you're going to end up in your eighty-five-year-old body reminiscing on . . . work. Is that the life you want to live?

I challenge you (and myself) to step out of the monotony of grinding to the bone and stepping into the present moment and just enjoying a bird's song or a child's laughter, or your spouse's silly jokes.

It's a practice. It doesn't just magically happen overnight. But it's worth it.

It's the in-between moments that make for a rich life.

With love,

Lindsay Maxwell

Not everyone has the same heart as you do.

Sooooo . . . how are you feeling with all of this topsy-turvy that's been happening since, oh, you know, March 2020?

It's overwhelming, isn't it?

Both sides too.

The blame, fear, reality, sacrifices, misinformation, data, losses, and division have been rather all-encompassing.

I am not on this planet to judge you. Or you, me. But I know deep down it's human nature to form our judgments, and we feel energy attached to it.

At this age, I tend to live my life in peace with peaceful people, and the people who have different factoids in their pockets, I personally am not here to try to change them, though sometimes not everyone quite has the same heart.

There is a lot of anger out there right now. Anger has never really been my "go-to." What's underneath anger? Sadness? Fear? Unjustness? Unmet expectations?

I try to deal with the source, not the surface.

And guess what, my faithful readers? You *all* feel as though you are right. Each and every one of you. And at this stage in the game, no matter what facts and truths and data you are shown, nothing short of a miracle will change that for you.

So I pose the question . . .

Are you going to live in harmony with others or ostracize your opponent?

What would your highest and most noble self do?

I leave you in peace, brothers and sisters, with that thought today.

Love,

Lindsay Maxwell

So . . . when's it going to be enough?

Seriously. What's it going to take for you to be satisfied?

Will it occur when everyone starts to think like you and do as you do, never to contradict or oppose? No.

Will you be satiated when things become perfect like abracadabra? Doesn't happen.

News flash. World peace isn't going to exist in our lifetime. Nor our children's lifetime. And this statement is coming from me—the eternal optimist!

That is because we live in an imperfect world filled with imperfect people and sometimes a hostile environment.

And. It's. Out. Of. Our. Control.

Yes, we can and should do what we think is best and good and kind and healthy. That's a sane approach.

You have a life. Others do as well. Sadly, we will all perish. (However, I have faith in heaven, and I can't wait to float around on a cloud in paradise eating chocolate ice cream with chocolate sauce and chocolate chips day and night. Okay . . . I do that anyway minus the whole "floating on a cloud" bit.)

All I'm saying is this.

Don't wait for things to be seemingly perfect to live. We live among evil people. We live among the unjust and the unfair. We harbor pathogens, bacteria, fungi, and other unpleasantries 24/7. There are people who lie, cheat, and steal and get away with it.

This world is not for the faint of heart, no.

But, my dear friend and faithful reader, you didn't come down here to merely just exist now, did you?

I didn't think so.

Carry on. Keep living. Make a life for yourself while you are able. You don't need anyone's permission.

With all the love I can muster,

Lindsay Maxwell

We need each other.

I was shown over the weekend just how apparent that is. And yes, even with the division of opinions, facts, beliefs, and creeds, we still need to embrace one another and not shun.

The common denominator in all things is either love or fear. You (yes, *you*) came from love which is all things harmonious. It allows you to work with others and be productive to create, not destroy.

Fear can and will and *is* creating division, chaos, deep-rooted rotten seeds, and sadness.

You see it. I see it. It's very much real.

Sometimes I think that if I were captured by aliens and placed alone or in isolation for a number of time, how would I feel upon seeing a familiar face of the human race? I would be joyous. No matter what faith they had or how right or wrong they were from my perspective views.

We need each other, kids. We aren't meant to do this alone. I will not tolerate a divide-and-conquer mentality while I'm here.

Sure, there are people whom I won't really want to send a Christmas card out to; but at the end of the day, each one of us is valuable and purposeful.

I hope this lands in your soul.

Love,

Lindsay Maxwell

You will totally tell that I am an '80s kid by what I'm about to say . . .

I received an image on my heart the other day.

Remember, in these trying and uncertain times with *everyone* feeling as though they are right, let me remind you that lack of hope creates fear. And fear creates hate. And hate promotes division. Be aware of that.

Let's get on with the image I got, shall we?

Mindfully taken from an excerpt of the movie *The NeverEnding Story* (context: G'mork was the scary wolf who was trying to kill Atreyu, the hero of the story):

G'mork: Foolish boy. Don't you know anything about Fantasia? It's the world of human fantasy. Every part, every creature of it, is a piece of the dreams and hopes of mankind. Therefore, it has no boundaries.

Atreyu: But why is Fantasia dying, then?

G'mork: Because people have begun to lose their hopes and forget their dreams. So the Nothing grows stronger.

Atreyu: What is the Nothing?

G'mork: It's the emptiness that's left. It's like a despair, destroying this world. And I have been trying to help it.

Atreyu: But why?

G'mork: Because people who have no hopes are easy to control; and whoever has the control . . . has the power!

Atreyu: Who are you, really?

G'mork: I am the servant of the power behind the Nothing. I was sent to kill the only one who could have stopped the Nothing. I lost him in the Swamps of Sadness. His name . . . was Atreyu.

Atreyu: [*The ground shakes again, and Atreyu is knocked down. He grabs a knife-shaped piece of broken stone and stands up, ready to fight.*] If we're about to die anyway, I'd rather die fighting! Come for me, G'mork! I am Atreyu!

PS. Atreyu wins.

My dear friends, do not allow "the Nothing" to spread in any of your minds, whatever you feel is right for you, humanity, your family, your faith, and your truth.

We must care for one another. We must love and unify. God, I'm such a hippie at heart (minus the whole patchouli scents and lack of shaved armpits).

The collective sickness is the swamps of sadness in our hearts. Let's fill "the Nothing" with goodness.

Sending love to each and every soul out there,

Lindsay Maxwell

Love your enemies.

Wow. I went there.

Come with me. The water is warm over here.

You can loathe what people do. You can feel strongly that there are rights and wrongs and even evils (which there sure are in this beautifully melancholic world of ours).

However, in order to be free, we must love our enemies.

Why?

Vile hate and anger promotes more vile hate and anger.

Love begets love. Love vanquishes and extinguishes darkness. And the cherry on top? It frees your heart.

Did you know that evil people aren't sitting there wringing their hands with a diabolical laugh exclaiming how evil they are (think Dr. Evil from *Austin Powers*)?

No.

Evil people feel totally justified in their wrongdoings for whatever self-serving fulfillment they are seeking. They do not think of their neighbors. They do not care about the betterment of humanity. They may even come across as charismatic and a "savior" of some sort. (PSA: Stay far away from those if you have an inkling that they are of that nature.)

Energy doesn't lie. People's hearts and souls emit a frequency. And the more gratitude, forgiveness, understanding, love, patience, and kindness that dwell in your heart will spill over and slowly enhance the world. Don't let darkness win by giving in to the hate and chaos that can sometimes surround us.

On your deathbed, you probably won't care who was right or wrong or this or that. You will care if you were kind and fulfilled your brilliant mission while here on Earth to bring sustainable joy and impact to others.

Is it your job to do so? No.

Do you have to? No.

But I tell you. Life is more peachy keen when you are not filled with vile bile.

Continue on from here.

Love,

Lindsay Maxwell

Sometimes I wonder what it's like on "the other side" of this lifetime.

I believe in heaven, so that's where my thoughts go:

In heaven, you will be with loved ones, have beautiful reunions, have no more tears, and have a purpose to shine brightly. You will be eating all the cake and ice cream calorie free for eternity, and, the cherry on top, you will be in the presence of God.

Sounds fab, right?

Well, why can't we bring that down to Earth right now? (I know the cake and ice cream morning, noon, and night just ain't feasible; so that will have to wait. Le sigh.)

I know not everyone on here believes in heaven.

However, I know you good people believe in good.

And I know that if you could have it your way, you would want a world of peace, loved ones surrounding you, less tears, and to shine bright.

So I pose this question: why don't we invite a little more kindness, wholesomeness, and goodness into our Earth home while we are here?

Slow down a little bit. Have meaningful conversations with friends. Cease gossip and slander. Be joyful for someone else's joy. Support. Encourage. Bear good fruit.

Look, I am not your mama. I have zero interest in telling you what to do.

But my blogs have a theme each week, and I have been closing them with gentle encouragements for years.

So, my friends, reflect on the good in your world. Invite more of that into your life. Let it stay for supper and a sleepover, even!

You will soon find that your life will bit by bit become more of what it was designed to be.

We could all use a little more goodness in our lives, dontchathink?

Rat-a-tat-tat.

Love,

Lindsay Maxwell

You are right.

See? You knew it all along, didn't you?

What I observe of us humanoids is that we totally feel justified in our beliefs. We each come from different backgrounds, belief systems, creeds, upbringings, educations, etc.

It all leads us to our personal experience with others and the world around us and even the world within us.

Two completely differently people can look at the same exact thing, and because of their individual perspectives, they can observe it to be different than the others' opinion.

This is not a new discovery. It has been common knowledge since the dawn of time.

I pose the question, though: what do you do when you feel adamant about something and the other feels adamant about the same something but it opposes your adamancy?

Do you argue and quarrel? Do you try to convince them that they're wrong? Or do you give the other person grace and accept where they're at?

I try to choose the latter. Because at the end of the day and at the end of my life, my relationships with people go far beyond the kindergarten mindset of who is right and who is wrong.

We can and should learn from one another. We each possess knowledge and nuggets of wisdom to impart. Let's not be ignorant that there are *always* two sides to a story and perspective.

But let me remind you, young grasshoppers, grace and class and patience will far exceed rash and fiery anger.

I bid you all a good day, and I hope that my words find you well.

With love,

Lindsay Maxwell

What is your end goal?

I've always had a knack for human nature. Between my careers in acting and hairstyling, I feel as though it aided me in tapping into the human spirit. I'll share with you now . . .

When you sat in my hairstyling chair, you poured your heart and soul out to me. You told me things in confidence that I will keep guarded for the rest of my life. You were real. You were safe. (And your hair was fabulous, if I can say so myself.) I saw you.

I saw you when you were homeless. I saw you when you teetered with leaving your spouse. I saw you blush when you saw how pretty you are. I saw you when you got diagnosed with cancer. I saw you when your husband passed away in his sleep. I saw you when you were getting your first haircut and when you graduated from high school. I cut your hair in silence while you prepared for your daughter's funeral . . .

I saw you. I get you. And I would never try to change you (except your hair color).

Then . . . there are the film scripts.

The people in imagination who exist through words, and I was fortunate enough to be the conduit to portray a glimpse or a chapter or a season in their life.

And it gives me great love and empathy for humankind. It's through the looking glass that I get to feel what it's like to be another person whom I don't have to like, even. But even when I channeled coldhearted schemers, I still tried to find their "why."

Imagine if you can give the gift of understanding. If you could bestow upon a person who may have a different set of beliefs that you so vehemently oppose a snippet of good will and an ear. If you could give enough space to another so that they feel free to process their authenticity around you. Imagine if you could loosen the grasp of your "unwavering opinion" to accept that we all have different perspectives yet we all want to feel special, loved, and heard.

So I beg the question: what is your end goal?

I'll let you in on a wee secret—kindness is classy.

And this world needs to smarten up in that department a little bit.

Love,

Lindsay Maxwell

I did laundry the other day.

Riveting news once again, I know.

However, as we know, my musings are usually spawned from the ever so mundane woven within my wee moments.

You see, I laundered my bathrobe, and the sash that was attached to it was all knotted and twisted upon taking it out of the dryer.

Of course it was.

It just went through topsy and turvy and to and fro to get to that state.

Of course it got me thinking about when you are in turbulence and your environment is in upheaval you can wind up all "knotted" up.

Sometimes our outside circumstances can deeply affect our fabric and general well-being. The tumble and turmoil that we experience on the outside can impact the twists and turns of our heart on the inside.

So knowing this and seeing this, I did what any Good Samaritan would do—I gently worked at the knot until it loosened and became untied.

I took full responsibility and dedicated time and patience to unravel the knot in my sash.

It would have fit the same, sure, and I could have even gotten by with the knots.

However, I know that I would always feel them and be aware of them.

I could tolerate it, yes, but is that what life is about? Just tolerating?

Nope.

My gentle encouragement for you this week is to pay attention to the little niggles and knots in your fabric of life. Yes, you can tolerate them. But if you have the power to eradicate them, why *not* untie the *knot*. #seewhatididthere

Always a play on words for the theatrics of it all.

Love,

Lindsay Maxwell

Not everyone likes me. Shocking, I know.

And not everyone likes you (which I personally cannot fathom because if you're reading this, I think you're rather swell).

Up until a couple of years ago, I gave too much energy and thought to being liked and amicable for all to enjoy.

I think we all have fallen victim to that personality trait on some accord.

I mean, I admit that I do not want to buy Christmas presents for *everyone* whom I cross. But I do try to find something I like about them because I believe that we all come from God and are made in the image of God: love, harmony, kindness, goodness.

However, we are human, and we have icky and gross qualities at times. We have judgments and envy and slander and piety and selfishness and narcissism and rudeness.

So much of the above mentioned, though, come from our disconnect from who we are meant to be in the light of where we come from.

My gentle encouragement for you is to connect back to that beautiful and radiant and loving gem that you are. Take a walk in nature. Go to a church service. Do some affirmations alone in your room. Whatever tickles your fancy. You know what that will do? It will start to awaken you to liking things just a bit more.

Stop being so cute, y'all.

Love,

Lindsay Maxwell

You are not too much.

Nope.

Even with all your big feelings, requests, desires, dreams, goals, ambition, drive, mini tantrums, failures, expectations, and the dynamic way you express yourself at times. No. You are not too much.

You see, we are darn fortunate to have the capacity to possess creativity, knowledge, intuition, self-expression, artistic talent, and all that jazz. We have so much within.

Somewhere along the line, though, something within us or in our developmental environment decided that we needed to play small or smaller than what our magnificent spirit is capable of.

We are confined to our bodies, yes, but sometimes don't you feel like you could burst out from yourself and bubble over?

There is nothing wrong with taking up space. There is nothing wrong with having a presence and leaving an impact and making your mark.

You are here for your time slot. You are here, and you are now.

This life is short. You are abundant and merry and sometimes dramatic and overbearing.

It's okay.

You belong here. You have purpose. You have production. You have a voice.

Use yourself.

Love you.

Lindsay Maxwell

Express yourself.

You see, I had an ugly cry the other day.

I was alone and listening to my existential crisis playlist, and I lay down on my hardwood floors by my window, and the sun was streaming through the glass, and my tears coincided with the stream of the sunshine.

It came on full force. I tried to examine it because, in my personal realm, my life is coming up roses. Truly. And gratefully.

I am healthy, my family is healthy, I have dear friends, and I am experiencing the greatest love I have ever witnessed. And I do not take one iota of that for granted.

But the world, you guys. It's getting tough out there . . .

I know since the beginning of time that every generation must have felt this at some point. Are we progressively getting worse?

My heart mourns for it all.

Sometimes I go quiet in the public eye because it's just too painful to talk about it.

I see it. I feel it. I empathize and engage with it.

And I know you feel it as well.

This blog is for you a little extra today. I am present to sit with you in your headspace. I get it. You are so not alone. Life can be a combination of beauty and heartbreak.

Also, sometimes we just need to allow our bodies to be the conduit for the emotions that flow through this wee ol' world of ours.

Cry. Laugh. Stomp your feet. Sing. Dance. Twirl. Write. Sleep. Talk.

Just express. It's okay to feel and to expel.

Love you,

Lindsay Maxwell

I added a little bit of extra salt to my pasta dish the other day.

Riveting, I know.

You see, when I placed all of the ingredients together, the sauce tasted perfect. But then I added the sauce to the noodles, and the taste of it just blandly blended in with each other. Therefore, I added salt.

With that, a musing was birthed.

Stick with me, kid, I'm going somewhere with this.

I added the salt to enhance the flavor and bring out the myriad of tastes that this dish had.

It got me thinking about our "salty" moments in life.

I'm not one to go looking for drama, but in my forty years of dwelling on this planet, I do have a bit of insight into life.

Sometimes we *need* a bit of contrast to shake up our routine. If everything flowed perfectly fine and we just tra-la-la'd our way through life, we would probably settle with complacency and her cunning cousin, idleness.

And *sometimes* that contrast can be a little too salty, and it leaves a bad taste in our mouths, so you adjust the recipe next time (kind of like learning from your mistakes?), and you move on accordingly.

Life is weird. And fabulous. And boring. And heartbreaking. And beautiful. And adventurous.

We weave in and out of the traffic flow with bumps, green lights, sights to see, and sometimes accidents along the way.

My loving encouragement for you this week is to be mindful of the amount of salt you put into your world. You don't need too much, but a little dose will do you some good.

You're doing well.

Love,

Lindsay Maxwell

I love seeing your joy.

Genuinely.

I want you to share your wins and triumphs with the world.

I want you to tell us what you had to go through to get you where you are. I want you to know that it is perfectly lovely for you to shine.

I want you to tell us that you feel fit, that you love your jiggle, that you are having a good mascara day, that you just learned a new word in a different language, that you finally got over your crummy ex, that you discovered that you were right along . . .

I want to you to scream your fantastical notions from the top of your lungs.

You see, misery loves company; and bonding over that, and only that, can become some deranged addiction.

I am not saying that we are not to walk in sorrow together or live in some sort of weird "Pleasantville" . . . because that would be unrealistic and odd.

However, let's shift our focus and get out of our ruts and start spreading good news for a change. It doesn't have to be life-altering event. But at the end of the day, it's all about finding the little joys in life. They are just as easy to find as the miseries in life. Your choice.

Love your fashionable faces,

Lindsay Maxwell

Keep it classy.

Yes, I know. Life can be messy and unkempt at times. There are definitely days when we aren't our best selves. We have brokenness, ugliness, and stuff that come up within that we ourselves don't like. (Don't even get me started with some of my past "hangry" behaviors).

We have choices in our actions toward our emotions.

We all have heated moments, and sometimes they can be overwhelming. We are passionate human beings; and I know for certain that there are times when our feelings, opinions, viewpoints, and expressions get the better of us.

Why don't we all take a moment or two for this gentle and much-needed reminder this week? Visualize here with me for a moment:

When someone or something boils your blood and you want to scream bloody murder at them, picture yourself as your highest, most regal, best state and take a step back and refrain.

You may just save yourself from regret, grief, festering anger, and deeper sorrow.

Emotions are real. Flowing through them is real too.

Yet this world has been too quick to judge, get angry, and get nasty as of late. Is that who we truly are? No. It's not.

Let the sunshine in. Then beam it out, Scotty.

You're a real shot of life, friends.

Love,

Lindsay Maxwell

I talk to trees.

No, I haven't gone off the rocker (I hope).

But I talk to trees. I mentally chat with them, and I send love to them.

I do that with strangers too. Sometimes I will walk down the street and send a little heart beam of love to them.

Why?

Because energy has weight. And let's face it, we all need an extra dose of love right now.

It starts with you. You have a certain responsibility to the energy you project to others. It's contagious too. Probably the most contagious thing out there.

So, my darlings, my encouragement for you this day is simple. Gather up all your goodies and hand them out to others.

It is your birthright to give and to serve.

Can I get an amen?

Love,

Lindsay Maxwell

There are rules in this playground of ours.

We were given this beautiful world to enjoy. We get to grow food, pet animals, climb trees, make friends, fall in love, sculpt art, swim in the ocean, and, now with modern technology, drive cars.

There is so much to do and so many people on our planet to do it with.

But what happens if we just run amok? What happens if we all think that *we* are right and you must follow *our* rules? We would have a circus for a world, wouldn't we?

I think we can *all* agree that we have different feelings, viewpoints, experiences, educations, tolerances, needs, wants, and desires, even if we are similar in spirit.

I don't know that we as humans have particularly succeeded on how to live in peace and harmony with one another. Since the dawn of time, history has repeated itself even when we think we have learned from our ancestors' unknowingness.

I desire peace. I desire harmony. And I would like to think you do as well.

So what shall we do about this?

My gentle encouragement for you is to be more compassionate with one another. If you see something on social media that makes you feel not so great, don't be so quick to judge or lash out. We are all coming from our own pasts and navigating through this little life together. Kindness, love, and patience go much further than your current mindset can properly comprehend in the heat of moments.

Thank you for joining me today.

Love,

Lindsay Maxwell

I was ten years old when an eccentric elderly man approached our table at a restaurant that my family was eating at.

He had a twinkle in his eye and looked directly at my brother and me and stated, "Fear is the enemy. Do not let fear ever stop you in life. There is nothing worse than fear."

He then sauntered off and never to be seen by my eyes again.

Well, eccentric elderly man, you weren't wrong.

Sure, there are natural and rightfully so fears (ahem, spiders . . . creepy little creatures).

What I think our old chap wanted to convey to us bairns was that we are to push through fear and not let us ever be controlled by it.

We will lose too much *life* if we are in fear. And it's a crippling downward spiral.

My encouragement for you is to face some fears, whatever that may look like for you. Feel it, yes, but push through against it. See how you feel after that.

Thank you to the white bushy-haired, weather-worn-faced, twinkly-eyed magic man for your message that day. Thirty years later, I have not forgotten you, and your message is shared today.

Love,

Lindsay Maxwell

You can get quite sassy when you are angry.

Well, that went sideways, didn't it? Hahaha.

I get it, though. In my past I used my tongue as a weapon of self-defense (it's probably most likely because I'm well in tune with the fine art of language). In my matured years, I have learned the other fine art of not escalating to anger. The years have a mellowing elixir, methinks.

The anger that we feel within these days are pretty valid and real. However, I had to drop into it and examine and process it.

Ready to go for a ride?

Okay. In my journey, I have been angry at what I deem to be absurdities and obvious unethical and unjust behaviors. (PSA: I have been all of the above and more, so I'm not exempt—we all have our goods, bads, and uglies.) I was looking at the world of the wicked and feeling helpless trying to get people to see *my* point of view.

Which brings me to our current day.

While there are definitely things to be angry about, it cannot rule you. That is how evil wins. And remember, my beautiful little friends, I often write and convey to you that we are made of love, harmony, creativity, and beauty.

Your anger and my anger are exactly where the evil wants to take us. And love will always rule over hate.

Sometimes I'm gentle with my encouragements, but today I'm going to give you an extra nudge. I challenge you to let go of the anger. I'm choosing to give it to God. Since the dawn of time, we as human beings have tried over and over to make it a perfect world. As much as I want it, I know I can only do my part. And my part and responsibility is to love you all, see you all, forgive, repent, and try and try again.

I am not going to fix this world. Neither are you. But we can take responsibility for ourselves and love one another.

Don't forget how to love.

Up, up, and away,

Lindsay Maxwell

What are you choosing?

Are you choosing good habits, selecting friends who lift you up, filtering what goes into your mind, exercising your body, taking vitamins, practicing self-care, and putting love into your relationships?

Or do you choose to go down rabbit holes of drama, pollute your body, look for negativity, and stay in toxic relationships?

We are human. It's not always going to be sunshine and roses in our lives each day. We will have negativity and theatrics in our lives. We cannot get through this journey unscathed by it.

However, we do have our own personal responsibility to choose what we "digest."

What we figuratively feed ourselves is what will make us grow into.

If we focus too much on drama, it will beget more drama. If we look for hate and some things to be sour about, by golly, you'll find it.

If you flip that, however, it will have the same impact. If you go looking for the great in others, you'll start to see it. If you water your relationships and nourish them, they'll grow into a beautiful garden.

The platform of your life is love. Not fear.

When you operate from love, you see the extension of what that is all around you.

When you operate from fear, you'll see the extensions of that manifest around you.

So I pose the question: what do you choose?

My challenge for you is to start shifting your focus off of fear/negative-based narratives. That could mean filtering what you read. It could mean cutting back on fast foods and perhaps going for a walk and listening to your favorite song or delving into a good book or uplifting podcast.

We all have choices laid out before us and within us.

Spoiler alert:

It feels good to feel good.☺

Love your faces,

Lindsay Maxwell

My closet needs organizing.

Out of all the things I could share with you on this fine day . . . that's all, folks.

Ha. As you know, if you're an avid reader of my musings, it doesn't stop there because, in true Lindsay fashion, a musing happened to be birthed in my closet.

You see, the condo that I live in is pristine. It's clean. It's bright. It's in working order.

Everything placed in there was set with intention, interior designer inspired, hired helping hands, and a lot of thoughtful and mindful construction and decision.

But that one room with the door closed . . . it has just been a plain old closet harboring clothes and shoes and doesn't have any flair. I just don't know what to do with it.

Well, we are kind of like that, aren't we? We have a tendency to put our "best faces forward" and have those sides of us that we shut the proverbial door to. Why? Because they're boring? Messy? Not in tip-top shape? A work in progress?

We don't show our closets or spare rooms out of fear of it not being "perfect."

We are human. We are not going to be perfect. We are brilliant and kind and weird and emotional and special and talented and nerdy and neurotic and charismatic and shy and dreamers. But we are not perfect.

There is no "monster in your closet" that we haven't all at some point in our lives seen in ours.

My gentle encouragement for you is to lovingly accept all parts of you. You are a beautiful mess sometimes. And sometimes you've got all your ducks in a row. It's all temporary.

And the best part is, in any moment that you wish, you can tidy up that closet and organize it. Your gift to yourself is the gift of change if you want it.

See ya later, Closet Monster.

Love,

Lindsay Maxwell

Go for grace. Not for vengeance or self-righteousness.

We are human, and more often than not, it is hard to play out a scenario without our defenses in full force.

Emotions and feelings are always valuable, as are expressing them. However, what I have learned throughout my years (and humbly have had to relearn) is to act with grace, empathy, understanding, and acceptance.

Listen, we all want to be right. Nobody really enjoys conflict; and we feel let down when peers, friends, and loved ones differ in innate opinion than us, especially these days.

But this world is becoming far too hasty to judge and divide and to conquer one another.

We have limited time while we are here, but the time that we do have should not be rushed nor brash.

I am reminded on this day of what my beloved, Jesus, stands for:

Grace. Forgiveness. Love. Compassion. Kindness. Beauty. Meaning. Courage. Hope. Unwavering strength.

We are offered all of those same beautiful attributes in our own hearts and our own souls.

It is there for the taking.

Personally, I would rather dwell in those delights than some old cruddy emotion like hate, revenge, self-righteousness, and judgment. Seems much more fun to pour out joy than to spew and hiss with venomous hate. It *is* your choice.

My gentle encouragement for you is to sneak a peek into your heart and see where your thoughts are gravitating toward. If your heart is starting to fill with darkness, switch the light off to what is making it feel dark.

If your heart is full of light, sprinkle that around because we need that more than ever.

Evil is a slippery slope. It can take hold of you in the most crafty of ways.

Want to hear the good news, though?

Spoiler alert:

Love wins.

Love,

Lindsay Maxwell

I was lying in bed the other day.

A favorite pastime for me, indeed.

And instead of thinking what my day ahead looked like and what my to-do's were going to be, I scanned my heart and soul and posed the question to myself:

"What would make me feel good? Not just today but in life?"

Authentic talk coming right up.

I thought about nice things I can do for my body. Like make a giant yummy salad and eat it throughout the week. I can move this wee body of mine (get outta bed, Linz!).

I thought about how I want to censor negativity in my life. C'mon, there will always be negativity in our human experience, but what can I do to not add to that? Limit social media. Unfollow constant naysayers (we all have bad days, but some of y'all enjoy misery and the weird attention it brings to you).

I'm becoming more choosy whom I allow into my life. I nourish and nurture deep friendships based on love, respect, kindness, and like-mindedness purpose.

I thought about how I want to contribute and what my current purpose is and what I can do to follow that.

In my heart of hearts and with prayer, I feel as if it's to write. I love my acting career, but due to proximity and my circumstances at this time, I have placed it on a hiatus.

So I beg the question to you:

"What will make you feel good? Are you able to design your life and recalibrate? Or do you feel like you're erring to be stuck in a rut?"

I know it's hard to get out of your own head. Lord, I know.

But are we going to do something about it? Or are we going to let days, months, and our years glimmer past us?

The choice is ours. The actions are up to us.

We will have an end to this life. Let's fill it up while we can.

Love,

Lindsay Maxwell

I had a great sleep last night. I was out like a light.

And I awoke at 4:00 a.m. in the same exact position as I fell asleep in. I was quite uncomfortable. So I shifted my positioning, and I felt much better.

And with that, musing was born!

You see, if we stay in one position too long, we become numb and less nimble. It becomes harder to adjust our sails because, even though we are uncomfortable, we may not way to move because it's a level of discomfort that we can tolerate.

However, tolerating your way through life doesn't sound very appealing, does it? Nah.

On the other side of discomfort is change and growth and usually a pot of gold (or something like that). But you'll never know if you "sleep in the same position" throughout your years.

My challenge for you is to examine where you fall:

Are you comfortably numb? Are you shaking it up a bit? Or are you shifting gears so much that you're living life in the fast lane? There are no rights or wrongs, my friends.

Sometimes we even are doing all three in different areas of our lives at once. It is, however, important to be mindful so that you can adjust those proverbial sails accordingly.

Toot toot! Full steam ahead!

Love,

Lindsay Maxwell

I noticed a wee something this week.

Those who you thought were your biggest cheerleaders sometimes aren't.

So I propose the question: why not?

These are the ones that I have noticed don't "like" nor "comment" no matter how your content is—authentic, superficial, emo, deep, lighthearted, poignant, and/or from the heart. And it had been going on longer than just a mere weird year.

I shouldn't notice. But I do.

I wonder if they bad-mouth me behind my back and don't want to be found out that they actually agree with what I'm saying.

I wonder if they've been secretly wishing for me to hurt and be sad to somehow make themselves feel better about their lives.

Or maybe they just plumb don't like me.

I used to give wayyyyy too much power to what others thought of me. Now, in my forties . . . nope.

I care a bit. Because I'm human. But here I am. Living the most beautiful, purpose-driven life, with people who love me and I love back.

My encouragement for you may sound and look a bit different for you than previous:

Give. Zero. Hecks (you know what I *really* would be writing if I weren't trying to keep it PG).

This is your one wild, whimsical, beautiful, and neat li'l life.

Love,

Lindsay Maxwell

We all have an effect on people.

Sometimes I wonder how I affect you. I wonder if you just scroll through my musings based on who I am. It's fine if you do. Truly. I don't take offense because I know I will never be everyone's cup of tea. Even though I am a very robust earl gray. Not everybody loves Earl Grey.

I love the fact that we will never be able to please everybody. Truly. And if you try, to please everyone all the time, you will get very, very stuck.

I'm not all about selfish living, though. I do believe in villages and communities and thoughtfulness. I received a nice card in the mail the other day. A couple of weeks prior to that, one of my girlfriends knew that I was going through something, and she sent me a little care package. I have people checking in on me daily, and that is worth its weight in gold. I don't think that we were meant to be alone at all. But I do know that we are not meant for everybody, and that's okay.

I think baby being an actress, I always wanted to be everything for everyone in the right "part for everyone."

But at this time in my life, I know that that is impossible. I are you think I want that. In fact, I know that I don't.

I challenge you to recognize that you will have an effect on people, but regardless what you do, you are still going to shop in people's lives however they wish to view you. Some people, no matter what you do, please see you as a villain. Some people always see you as a saint. You are neither. You are human. Act accordingly.

Love,

Lindsay Maxwell

Stop it. Stop it right now. You care too much about what other people think. And guess what? It doesn't get you very far now, does it?

Oh, little ones, I have been so guilty of this in my past; and it still has the ability to weave its way into my psyche.

I was dancing to a David Bowie song yesterday. By myself. In my living room. I felt shy. I felt like if someone were to watch me, they would recognize that I have zero rhythm. But then I gave my head a shake and danced like nobody was watching. Because . . . nobody was. I felt so free and powerful and airy.

Which brings me to this.

No matter how bad or imperfect or not quite there you think you are, does it truly matter? And are you aware that every single darn human being who walks this Earth and has before and will again also has moments, seasons, and bouts of self-doubt?

I get it. Phrases, expressions, and opinions are now captured and frozen on this internet. It's easier to feel like you need to edit yourself and not live authentically. We have Facetune, and fears of saying too much or too little, and we have massive opinions from all walks of life. We have the way we perceive ourselves that may differ from what others see us as.

Phew. I'm getting exhausted even writing this.

Because, well, it is exhausting.

We do not have to be anything to anyone. Heck, we have the privilege to change our minds, thoughts, and opinions at any given time if we should choose.

This life is yours to create. It's not for me to look into your life. Nor you to mine. Give people space and let 'em be.

My challenge for you is to do something bold and out of your comfort zone. Even if it's small. Do it for you and let go of the worry attached to it if some bloke from your old high school has an uneducated "opinion" on it.

You're a wizard, Harry.

Love,

Lindsay Maxwell

You have the gift of feeling things that are unseen by the eye. We call that little ditty empathy.

You can feel it in the words that you read, in the conversations you have, and even the unspoken presence near others.

Energy doesn't lie.

Have you ever noticed that even when you get a text from someone who is upset but doesn't want to let on, somehow you can still feel that something isn't quite right? Or even if someone has a smile on their face, it doesn't quite match their eyes?

We are all composed of emotions, feelings, thoughts, and innate frequency. Each one of those adjectives is proven to emit energy.

When we go out into the world or converse with a spouse, loved one, or general public, where we are at with ourselves directly impacts the experience you will have with other people and your surroundings.

Obviously, we are not always radiating our sunshiny selves. It would be weird, like "Pleasantville." And hopefully, we aren't in perpetual doom and gloom. That too would be rather unpleasant(ville). Hehehe.

The experience we have out there has so much to do with what we are experiencing *in* there—within.

My encouragement for you is to have a little "check-in" with yourself. Are you tipping the scales erring on the habitual woeful side? Are you feeding that wolf too much? Or are you noticing some beautiful bloom and budding within?

Breathe. Be gentle with your progress. Be mindful that this world is here for your experience with it.

And for heaven's sake, remember that you are a fabulous little butterfly.

I certainly think you are swell.

Love,

Lindsay Maxwell

What are you taking for granted?

I ask that without intending to make you feel bad if there are certain things that just popped into your mind.

I only ask because recently I realized a few everyday things that I took for granted were temporarily stripped away from me over the recent weeks, and boy, it sure made me realize how delightful it is to have the mini joys of simplicity.

Okay. Back to it.

Listen, we have a billion little things to be grateful for. Yes, even in the era of trepidation.

We have mornings and evenings. We have longer and brighter days ahead. We have fresh socks and mascara. We have sourdough bread. We have funky umbrellas and books and pets. We have coffee and video games and online shopping. We have crossword puzzles and pickles.

You guys, we have it all.

My encouragement for you is to jot down five things that you are grateful for. It could be grandiose or itty-bitty life pleasures. What that will do to your brain is set it in motion to bring about more things *to* be grateful for.

Gratitude is your superpower.

Up, up, and away,

Lindsay Maxwell

How are you?

I tend to check in with that question from time to time. And I genuinely want to know how you're doing. Sometimes it's just plumb good to vent and unload.

There are days and moments where we haven't been well. And that is okay. This is one of the oddest times I personally have currently existed in, and if my circumstances were different than they were, who knows how I would be fairing?

So I pose the question to you: What measures your well-being? Health? Financial ease? Loved ones' thriving? Feeling productive? Connection?

I'm making you think today, aren't I?

I went through my existential crisis about ten years ago. Phew. Glad that's over with. I asked myself and reflected a lot about what my "purpose" was, and I want to share with you today if you are feeling stuck like I was.

The quiet and gentle answer was such:

To help. To serve. To provide something.

You see, it doesn't matter what role you play in that, but we are here to offer up what we have to others. It's one of the ultimate secrets to true peace.

You can help by calling a friend. You can help your neighbor with tedious tasks. You can open a door for a stranger or volunteer at a shelter.

My darkest moments in which I couldn't escape were the moments that my purpose was woven and embedded into me. Like you, I am here to serve in whichever capacity I can.

My encouragement for you is to step outside of your own head and story and reach out to someone. You'll build a connection. You'll build purpose. Your heart will expand.

You are more valued than you'll ever know.

Love,

Lindsay Maxwell

Today, I am going to talk about relationships.

Romantic ones.

It's something up often talked with my friends, colleagues, clients, family, and even partners I've had. But I don't often write about them. Because they are so subjective.

However, they are such a strong part of our lives that I want to touch on the subject matter this week. Have fun reading.

I am no guru on relationships. I know that if you've been friends with me long enough or have been on my Facebook long enough, you've seen some relationships that differ from my current. And out of respect, we will leave the past in the past.

Each connection I've had with every human being, including men, has been a lesson unto its own. My heart has always longed to find a connection with a soulmate. Ever since I was a little girl, I have desired connection with people.

I placed a lot of value in finding the perfect relationship for me. What I should have done, though (hindsight is always twenty-twenty) is I should have paid more attention to whom I was and whom I was going to become.

We live in a very different era now.

It's not so much just high school sweethearts getting married anymore.

There are divorces and breakups and separations and getting back together and remarriage.

I am no stranger to a broken heart. What I do know from my experience is that even though our hearts are so fragile, they are beautifully resilient. During my darkest days, I had so many people band together and protect me from getting too low.

But I don't mind the fact that my heart has been broken. Not at all. It was the greatest teacher in my life because it forced me to really look inward *and* outward, and it gave me strength and resilience that, unless I had that experience, I would not have grown into the woman that I love today.

This is not a diary entry.

I have done the work. Being the empath that I am, I have learned boundaries and how not to be codependent. If you have any further questions on that part of my journey and how I got to where I am today and any tips I can give you, my heart is always open to share privately.

It takes two to tango. Yes, in any relationship, either one can look like the bad guy. But I do know from experience that that's also subjective. People do bad things. People say mean things. People are damaged. And unless you do work, and I mean extensive work, it is very hard to have a thriving relationship. Especially in this world today.

And it's not always easy. I don't think anything great in life is supposed to be super easy. However, I don't think that it should be super hard either. Some of you may remember my smoothie analogy. If you are new to my page, I am going to share it with you. And for those of you who have heard this before, it's a great reminder.

I will leave you with this:

You are a tasty smoothie. You have all the wonderful flavors within you. You have all the nutrients, and you taste great on your own. A relationship should be your booster. Something that will just enhance your performance but is not needed to taste good. With this poster, you are just a better version of your own smoothie. The booster will never detract from you. It will only add richness and more flavor and more performance and a better consistency.

I love food, and this is why I equate most things to food.

There you have it, my friends. A little blip.

Kisses to your heart.

Love,

Lindsay Maxwell

You are about to boil and bubble over.

I see it. I feel it. I understand you to the extent I can. However . . .

The question is, what kind of ingredients within are going to spill out of you? What kind of dish are you going to serve? (And if you know anything about me, food metaphors are almost always integrated into my everyday speech.)

What are you putting into your big old cauldron of life? Nourishment? Rich spices and flavors? Real and whole elements? Robust textures? Sustainable life sources?

Or are you cutting corners and hastily adding synthetic ingredients? Are you mixing toxic substances, bland additives, second-rate useless muck?

In case you haven't caught on to my appetite for life (in more ways than one), my provoking question to you for this week is this:

Are you feeding that soul of yours life-enhancing goodies, or are you diminishing your soul by feeding it toxicity?

Life-enhancing goodies can range from self-care, patience, compassion, art, prayer, nourishing foods, fruit-bearing connection, servitude, and loving your neighbor.

Toxicity can range from fear, doubt, hate in your heart, judgment, smarminess, shame, indulging in too much negativity, gossip, and false narratives.

I get it, though. We are human. We attain beautiful ingredients and icky ones.

My encouragement for you is to ask yourself, what kind of meal are you serving to your guests? Are you nourishing them or depleting them? And as you nourish or deplete others, you are nourishing or depleting yourself.

Can't wait to see that magnificent creation of yours.

Love,

Lindsay Maxwell

I got a new phone the other day.

Riveting, I know.

However, in usual Lindsay fashion, it sparked up a musing within me.

You see, the picture quality is extremely clear and vivid. It's spectacular, actually.

And though this little morning musing is not an ad for a phone, it brought a little insight to this wee noggin o' mine.

I thought about what new and fresh energy can bring us. If we are to actually be present in the moment, instead of looking from our old perspectives and "lens," then we could see life as it is rather than our former habitual thinking.

We as humans are creatures of habit, and so often, that is why history often repeats itself. Whether it is repeating on a personal (continue dating the wrong person for you, always seeming to be stuck in a rut, feeling like you're living the same life since the '90s) scale or a global one (wars, massive events, corruption, destruction, etc.), the fact is that until we stop being our habits and looking out from our old lens, we will be blind to the beauty and brilliance of what we can create and is created all around us each day.

To look through a new lens, we must discipline (I know, I know—I loathe that word as much as you do) ourselves to take in the precious idiosyncrasies that this world and each moment have to offer. Have a deep and distraction-free conversation with a friend, look around your home at the colors in each room, focus on mindful breathing. Be intentional with words and thoughts you say to yourself.

Your life is short (sorry, but in comparison to the Great Eternal, it is). So *get out of your head!* Spring up and be alive! Be present. See the world through a fresh and unfiltered lens. Play. Each day holds magnitude and attitude within. Go toy around with it. Make it yours.

Adjust the lens.

Tallyho,

Lindsay Maxwell

I am thinking of two things right now. I'm thinking of my present and past.

Now, I am a huge advocate for trying to place our awareness in the present, yet I tend to turn and reflect upon my past once in a while.

Why?

Because I am so damn grateful for it.

The Lindsay I was a mere few years ago looks different than the Lindsay I identify with today. (Still blonde. Still 5'7".)

And . . . same with you.

Yes, you still possess your essence and quirks and interests and disposition. Yet you have grown.

You've gained a laugh line. You've earned that glint of wisdom in your eye. Your face now carries the loss of a loved one. Your strength has made you resilient. The weight of lack of self-esteem is slowly dissipating. You are shaping into what this present time calls for.

I was listening to a song the other day. About getting everything we want in life.

Heck no. Where is the fun and glamour and gravitas in that?

Sure, we love it when things work in our favor. It allows ease and flow. And I personally adore those feelings.

However, all the trials and tribulations and obstacles and hurdles you pushed through accumulate to make you exactly where and who you are right now.

It was worth it.

Don't argue with me. I have been in anguish before too. But, hot dang, it was worth it.

And if you aren't there yet, trust me, my darling friend, you will be.

And even when I didn't feel that it would be okay, I just knew it would be.

So, my tired and exhausted friends who are in a cycle—my message to you is this:

Hold on. It's a roller coaster. There are times when you're going to hold on for dear life and times where you flail your arms up in the air with glee.

The ride will one day end. You'll look back. You'll see that the parts that looked the scariest were the most exhilarating and that you will always go up and down and sometimes even upside down.

Don't fret. Close your eyes and scream it out. Open them to take a look around.

Spoiler alert:

It's going to be okay.

Love,

Lindsay Maxwell

The end is near.

Okay. Okay. Enough with the theatrics, Lindsay.

But . . . the end is near.

Which end, though? The end of self-doubt? The end of procrastination? The end of tirelessly putting others before you?

Everything. And I mean, everything, must come to an end at some point.

Even our most favorite moments eventually subsides.

And that's okay.

Because endings are followed by new beginnings. They're intertwined with growth and transcendence and understanding our nature and how we relate to others.

The end makes room for the start. And thus, the cycle begins.

In nature we have a beginning, a middle, and an end. And then we embark on a new cycle, a new season.

Yes, my friends, the end is near.

My challenge for you is to let go of what you're clutching so deeply to. Loosen that grip a wee bit.

Let it flow.

Reveling in your end and genuinely excited for your beginning,

Lindsay Maxwell

Things aren't always as scary as we make it out to be. Take my fear of flying, for example.

I used to get myself all revved up and in a tizzy *dreading* the takeoff only to board the plane and secretly wish that they'd hurry up and take off more quickly because I had to use the restroom.

I would quietly giggle to myself how I went through all that hype and anxiety for something that was just bred in my brain.

Now, I'm not here to diminish your fears and anxieties. I know how we all rationalize those to ourselves and have them for our reasons.

However, I want to remind you and myself that things aren't always exactly how they seem to us. And sometimes, sometimes, my dear friends, we can have collective fear and anxiety about the unknown.

My encouragement for you and myself today is to look at our dragons. Face them. Slay them if you will. They're not larger than you or me.

Slayyyyyyy.

Love,

Lindsay Maxwell

How long do you think you'll be here for?

Such a question, isn't it?

I am convinced that I am going to depart this Earth when I'm ninety-three years old on a Thursday in February. In fact, I even have the date marked on my iPhone calendar. (Thursday, February 8, 2074, to be exact. I came up with that ripe age to exit when I was about ten years old. Odd little child that I was.)

So now that you have that little ditty for your records, let's get back to the original question.

How long do you think *you* will be here for?

And what are you going to do with your precious time?

Are you going to seek knowledge? Are you going to fall in love? Are you going to have children and teach them miraculous things? Are you going to learn a language? Are you going to hop on a plane and go to a destination you want to go to? Are you going to stand up for yourself? Are you going to read books? Are you going to cry yourself to sleep? Are you going to owe in taxes? Are you going to bless a friend with a good deed?

There are many facets to being a human being. Joy, love, sadness, fear, trepidation, and curiosity can all coexist with each other.

Trust me.

I have tremendous joy within. I carry it around because I'm in tune with my innate nature. I also pick up pieces of worry and fragments of fear, I stub my toe on anger, and I flip my next page to curiosity.

This is our life. And though I only have fifty-three years left, I want to soak up all it offers and give what I can offer.

And I want you to as well.

My encouragement for you is to become aware that you won't be here forever (but don't dwell—there's another level after this game), and think about if it's time for you or not to start living the life you desire. It doesn't have to be monumental. It can be found in minute ways. The point is make the most of it. Have intention. Don't be a zombie. Open those beautiful eyes of yours and see the world and the people who surround you.

Wakey-wakey! Today is a new day!

Love,

Lindsay Maxwell

Misery loves company.

You have heard this phrase before.

I started to examine the phrase after reflecting on some things last night.

Have you ever had that friend who steers away from you when everything is going seemingly right in your life, but as soon as you mention something remotely negative, they're right there to complain and perpetrate even more negativity? And before you know it, you feel worse off talking to them than you did before?

Misery and pain are in our lives at times. Joy and exuberance are as well. We all measure our feelings by our nature and how they personally affect us and those we love.

However, your energy is contagious.

Have you ever noticed that person who walks into a room and you automatically feel like your mood has increased? And then there are some that can drain you and leave you feeling depleted?

The way I look at things is that our time here on Earth is limited. It truly goes by in a blip.

My encouragement for you is to be more mindful where you steer your energy toward. Have intentional thoughts. Yes, you will have moments of deep sadness, but you'll also have moments of deep gladness. Try to surround yourselves with people who enhance and enrich your life. That in itself is a game changer.

I get an email every day, and the tagline is such:

"If thoughts become things, choose the good ones!"

Choose your own adventure.

Love,

Lindsay Maxwell

I tried to jump into my television set when I was three years old.

I sometimes think I tell you too much.

I was watching *She-Ra and the Princesses of Power*, and She-Ra had light and magical powers shooting out of her hands.

Naturally, I wanted in on some of it, and I figured since I was little, I'd be able to fit into that TV box and obtain that beautiful and radiant light that she was pouring out of her cartoon hands.

It hurt slamming into that TV screen.

But I loved how I truly believed I would be able to succeed. "A" for effort.

Here I am, almost thirty-six years later (I'm turning thirty-nine for the first time in a couple of weeks . . . maybe not the last?), and I'm still awestruck by the magic I see in life.

You see, whether it was real or not, I truly believed it was. Yes, I know it was just a cartoon and make-believe. However, isn't it the belief in magic and love and creativity and joy that makes us go after our dreams?

And isn't it the dream of inventors, artists, engineers, and writers to create new possibilities that will slowly shift and guide us to new heights?

We are not meant to stay stagnant. We are meant to follow that whisper that we all have imprinted within us, grandiose or not.

We all have purpose. We are here to serve one another, love one another, take delight in the small things, soak up a little sunshine, and go through the human experience. There will be sadness. There will be hurt feelings. Heck, there might even be a few broken hearts along the way.

In the same breath of your life, there will also be exuberance, thrills, giggles, treats, and deep belly laughs.

The magic is all around us and within us.

I see it in you. I see it in me. I see it in tea, even. Which reminds me . . .

It's time for tea.

Your show must go on.

Love,

Lindsay Maxwell

I have been wrong once or twice. Maybe thrice.

The horror!

And you have been wrong at times too.

Even more horror!

That being said, once we are shown the truth backed up by what life is offering up to us and showing us what's really going on around us and people showing their true colors, well, then, it's our responsibility to admit, "Hey, maybe I believed my own narrative for this long, and a lot of other people believed in it as well. However, something just isn't right, and I don't feel right about believing, practicing, or being involved with this anymore."

Our egos and false narratives are mind traps. They are our habits and facsimiles that we replay over and over in our heads. We tend to hold on tight to them because we feel that is our identity.

I'll speed up the process for you: your ego and habits are not your identity. At all.

We are made to live in each moment. We are allowed to learn, grown, obtain new information, let go of what we no longer deem to be true, and shed some past ideologies.

The trouble lies within holding on to something or someone that really bears no good fruit, yet we hold on because at one point it brought comfort and familiarity to us.

We could get so caught up in believing something so strongly that is no longer relevant nor true and actually have light shed on the truth about someone or something, that we don't *want* to see it or believe it because we would feel like we let ourselves down or that we were somehow a fool.

No. You are not a fool and weren't a fool. But it would be considered foolish to hold on to something you know in your very soul that is not correct nor good for you.

I do not know where each one of you is at in your self-awareness level. Or your awareness of other people's psyches, the way collective consciousness works, or even where you are spiritually.

However, I do know that if you are reading this, you have a soul and a brain and intuition.

So my encouragement for you is to trust in that a wee bit more. If something feels off (like spiders, ugh), it probably is.

Forward is the only way,

Lindsay Maxwell

Have you looked in the mirror today?

I have.

And did you spend too much time zeroing in on all the little imperfections you deem to be, well, imperfect? Well, let me set us straight (because I do that as well).

If you've been a follower of my musings for a while, about every year or so I write about body image and our relationship to our bodies.

I often spout off about how fortunate we are to have eyes to see, limbs to prance, lungs to breathe, and a tongue to make verbal noises with.

It's a pretty neat thing to occupy a body while living on this Earth.

However, I know how we think. No matter our shape, size, fitness regimen, goals, genetic makeup, and health quotient, we all have moments of feeling inadequate in our bodies.

So I'm here to walk with you and dissect it alongside each other.

Whichever way you want to look at it, this is our physical home from birth to death.

Some of us are born with all our limbs working. Some of us are not. Some of us endure accidents, and we lose parts and mobility. Some of us develop diseases. And some of us can smoke like a chimney and drink like a fish and outlive others.

The conclusion I came to after scoping my body out at its current state is that it's mine.

It's mine to play hide-and-go-seek with. It's mine to kiss my lover's lips with. It's mine to hug you with. It's mine to stretch. It's mine to cry. It's mine to bathe.

It truly is the greatest instrument I will ever own.

We have all endured hardships, illnesses, stresses, flus, loud sneezes, and heartaches. That is part of the human experience.

I challenge us to look at our bodies. Embrace the jiggles or the protruding bones or your lumps and bumps and stretch marks. Don't get mad at your left hand at being slightly smaller than your right. That dimple when you smile? Adorable! That longer middle toe? They say it means good luck! You are uniquely you.

Keep moving the best you can. Eat your veggies. Have cake. Drink plenty of water. Have a glass of wine if it suits you and enjoy the ride.

You sexy thang, you.

Love,

Lindsay Maxwell

My dad has a garden. He's been tending to it for more than twenty-five years.

And when I say garden, I'm talking acres of land, a gazebo, a yard, rolling hills, and even a putting green.

It's his pride and joy (other than my mama and us kids and his grandkids).

He sent me a recent photo of it the other day. As familiar as it looked as it's still the same home I grew up in, I noticed the differences, the growth, the added beauty, and the care put into it.

I thought of the future. I thought of many years from now, after he is gone (or he will probably live forever . . . oh, how my heart wishes this), how the yard and garden will have a life of their own and all of the care, love, devotion, and etching will still echo him.

And, in proper Lindsay format, I thought to myself how the mirrors what we tend to in our lives, namely, the relationship we have with people.

When we nurture, tend to, love, devote, pour into, and be patient with our loved ones, by golly, they sure bloom, do they not?

I know we are in this crazy little world. I know it's not always coming up roses, and there are weeds to pull and grass to water and seeds to plant.

At the end of the day, beautiful flowering and blooms come from a mixture of hard work, perseverance, consistency, love, patience, and trusting.

Just like our relationships.

My encouragement for you is to treat your loved ones with care. Watch them shine and grow as you do.

You'll be glad you did.

With love and life,

Lindsay Maxwell

If I ever go looking for my heart's desire again, I won't look any further than my own backyard. Because if isn't there . . . . I never really lost it to begin with.

—Dorothy Gale *(The Wizard of Oz)*

In light of this classic and beloved movie's eightieth anniversary, I would like to delve into that above statement.

So often we feel as though there are bigger and better adventures and experiences and people and riches out there. We seek foreign land, new beginnings, shedding of our pasts; and all too often, we run.

Yes, there is a vast world out there. Yes, we are meant to explore. I thoroughly encourage it.

But, dear reader, if you are looking to exterior things to fill a void in your life that you haven't confronted or looked at in yourself, you will be a slave to this world.

This world is ever changing, and our perception of life is too. There is something to be said of consistency and foundation.

There is an elusive dragon out there that some of us try to chase. We think it will provide the next best thing, yet when we "catch it," we soon find another elusive dragon to chase. Therefore, we spend our lives not satisfied by what we currently have here and now.

I am not suggesting that we stay stagnant, no. I am, however, suggesting that we take a look at our home and values around us and stay close to the consistency and beauty that we come from.

My encouragement for you is to take in a deep breath and look at your life. Look at what you have. Do you have a home? Do you have family? Do you have a good friend? Do you have love? Do you have air in those lungs of yours?

You lucky duck. You do!

I encourage you to appreciate those riches that you have and that have built your foundation.

You know I have to say it . . .

Because . . .

There's no place like home.

Love you all just as you are,

Lindsay Maxwell

"I know what is needed."

I wrote those words to a dear friend last week.

You see, they were going through deep heartache. They were at the lowest of the trenches of despair.

Unexpected. Offside. Curveball. Betrayal. The whole shebang.

I knew what to share with them in that moment. I knew I wasn't there to fix it. I knew that I was not to give advice. I was there to sit, to listen, to be present.

We are meant to receive and give in this short and sometimes melancholy life we live. And when it's time to give our presence and comfort, it truly is our time to give.

The only reason I knew what was needed was because once upon a time(s), I needed it myself.

My encouragement for you is to take your run at the role that you play in others' lives. Perhaps be a friend and a confidant. Offer up your space. Be a safe energy. Listen. Hold their grief and woe gently in your proverbial arms.

You never know what the heartbreak you have endured in your past will be turned into support for others and was not used in vain. It is one of our greatest teachers.

With deep empathy,

Lindsay Maxwell

I will never leave you; never will I forsake you.

—Hebrews 13:5

Grab your coffee/tea and come on a journey with me.

When I was a youngster, I had an innate fear of abandonment. My wee soul was so worried about being left behind or alone. It was a slight irrational fear because I had doting parents and a brother and sister whose presence was always abundant. I had friends, teachers, and extended family who all outpoured love.

However, it didn't stop that niggling feeling that something bad may happen at any time.

I don't think I've ever gotten to the root of it; chalked it up to having it woven into my sensitive nature, perhaps.

Now, in my adult years, of course I have experienced loss, disconnection, abandonment, dissolution of relationships, etc.; and sometimes it felt just as terrible as my young self imagined it would.

Those are chapters in my proverbial book that are written on my heart and kept to close conversations only. I navigated through them. I prayed. I leaned on. I surrendered. And I healed.

Today I want to share with you this:

You are never alone. Ever.

Also, do not place too much faith in mankind. I'm not a pessimist by any means. Quite the opposite, I would say. However, mankind is fickle, and we are all on our little roller coasters of life, and each one of us is going at it at our pace, and we each are perfectly imperfect. Reliable? At times. But not one of us should put that kind of pressure on another human being for their joy and happiness.

My encouragement for you is to quiet down a bit. Break the cycle of your every day. Turn off the news, stop engaging banter on social media, and bow out of the rat race—even if it's just for a bit. Carve out a moment or two to be alone with your thoughts and hear what is to be said.

You are so amazing. You are so loved. Beyond measure, my friend.

With love,

Lindsay Maxwell

I watched a show last week, and one of the characters passed away unexpectedly.

It stayed with me.

I know that is a sad reality for most of us here to have someone we dearly love pass away and leave us, whether it be unexpected or prolonged, but it doesn't take away from the impact that each passing imparts.

I just read a beautiful thing that helped, though.

(Also, I believe that I will be going to heaven when I pass and eat ice cream with Jesus with all the fixings, but I know not all of y'all believe in that, but if you ever have questions, I'm here for you. About Jesus. Not really ice cream. Because I ate it all.)

Your soul will learn about mysteries and beauty and truths the way it just cannot here on this earthly realm. Yes, we have miracles and wonders all around us now at any given moment, but just think about how beautiful and all-encompassing it will feel. Answers will be revealed. We will be reunited. And it will be more than we could ever imagine.

We will all transition away from what we know one day. It's a sobering thought, indeed. And I am no stranger to death of loved ones and the grief it delivers. However, in my great walk in this life, I want to remind you just how fleeting time is and how rich, even the smallest and mundane, the music notes of life can be.

My gentle encouragement for you today or even this week is to ask yourself deep and soul-baring questions. I know that this season and life as of late can be riddled with anxiety and focus on just getting through the day.

But, my fine friend, remember why you are here. Remember what your grand purpose is (spoiler: to love). And remember that your time is short by standards of eternity and that you, my dearest, are important to the master plan.

With a spoonful of ice cream to help you swallow today's musing,

Lindsay Maxwell

Have you ever believed and held on to a belief so tightly to one day find out that you were believing in something that wasn't true? Relationships? Self-limiting beliefs? World affairs? Career opportunities?

Like Santa? (Just kidding, he's real. Phew!)

But really, there have been many times that I was *so certain* in something because of either the narrative around it/them, how I felt about it, or even the illusion it gave me was so convincing that it just had to be true.

And I know that I'm not the only one.

Once I found out that I wasn't privy to all the facts and truth and "man behind the curtain," was I humbled? Yes. Did I fully accept that I could have been foiled or bamboozled? Noooooo . . . because don't "I" have innate discernment? Wouldn't we be able to tell a falsehood from a truth?

Well, not necessarily. And I'll tell you why.

You are living in your reality. You come from your lineage, upbringing, environment, diet, self-awareness, core beliefs, peer influences, and choices you've made along the way.

I come from my reality with a myriad of the above but differing from yours.

What feels to be true to me in my core being may feel completely wrong in yours.

So who is right and who is wrong? Is it even about that?

Do you think this maybe is why we can't get off the hamster wheel of "he said/she said" so easily and so quickly these days?

Look, I know what's up. We are born, we live, and then our earthly bodies perish. Each and every one of us.

Life is a calling for you to experience the flow of it and not be in constant battle mode all the time (unless you play Mario Kart and enjoy that option).

My encouragement for you is to *puh-lease*, for the love of God, unplug for a while from all the mayhem that's surrounding us. Outside influences can have this way of spoon-feeding us, but the deliverer is shoving it down our throats leaving us grasping for air. It's utterly exhausting at times, isn't it?

Hug a friend. Take a walk. Deep breathe. Wash away yesterday or last week or the past years. Your time may be up tomorrow, and I want you to enjoy this venture.

Your future self wants you to as well, you li'l rascal.

Always with love,

Lindsay Maxwell

I recognize a lot of people by the back of their heads.

I chalk it up to being a hairstylist for more than twenty years (alongside my acting career—what a life) and paying close attention to my art, which is the back of your head.

I was looking for someone in a crowd the other day and instead of trying to see their familiar face, I opted to look for the back of their head, and boom. I spotted them ever so quickly.

It's the way I do things.

And you have your own unique way of doing things.

You see, life is not a "one size fits all" or a place for conforming and following the masses. No.

There are twists and turns, and you choose your own adventure plots.

This is your one fragrant, impactful, silly little life.

My encouragement for you is to see how when you start to do things that align with your very soul, you start to observe how your world will suddenly become a truly wondrous place.

By the way, you have a gorgeous back of head.

Love,

Lindsay Maxwell